GHOST STORIES
of
TEXAS

Jo-Anne Christensen

Lone Pine Publishing

© 2001 by Lone Pine Publishing
First printed in 2001 10 9 8 7 6 5 4 3
Printed in Canada

The Publisher: Lone Pine Publishing

10145 – 81 Avenue   1808 B Street NW, Suite 140
Edmonton, AB T6E 1W9   Auburn, WA 98001
Canada   USA

Website: http://www.lonepinepublishing.com
            www.ghostbooks.net

National Library of Canada Cataloguing in Publication Data
Christensen, Jo-Anne.
    Ghost stories of Texas

    ISBN-13: 978-1-55105-330-1
    ISBN-10: 1-55105-330-6

    1. Ghosts—Texas. I. Title.
BF1472.U6C49 2001   133.1'09764   C2001-910463-4

Editorial Director: Nancy Foulds
Project Editor: Shelagh Kubish
Illustrations Coordinator: Carol Woo
Production Manager: Jody Reekie
Book Design: Arlana Anderson-Hale
Cover Design: Robert Weidemann
Layout & Production: Arlana Anderson-Hale

Photo Credits: The photographs in this book are reproduced with the generous permission
of their copyright holders. Austin History Center, Austin Public Library, PICA 05020
(p. 15); PICA 06530 (p. 39); C00193 (p. 83); C03705 (p. 123); PICA 03252 (p. 157); PICA
11450 (p. 170); C00192, (p. 198); C03861 (p. 207); Texas/Dallas History and Archives
Division, Dallas Public Library Image PA76-1/8949.1 (p. 55); Image PA85-39/21 (p. 107);
Image PA76-1/9708.2 (p. 115); Image PA82-00238 (p. 222); Richard Federici (p. 26).

We acknowledge the financial support of the Government of Canada through the Book
Publishing Industry Development Program (BPIDP) for our publishing activities.

PC: P1

Dedication

For William and Natalie,
who proved that things get
bigger when you even THINK
about Texas ...

Contents

Chapter 6: Haunted Houses

Chapter 7: A Strange Assortment

Acknowledgments

My name may appear on the cover of this book, but there are many kind and generous people who have contributed to its creation. I wish to take this opportunity to acknowledge them, and to offer my sincere gratitude.

To the management and staff of Lone Pine Publishing—your creativity, enthusiasm, professionalism and support continue to impress me. I am so pleased to be a part of what you do. A special mention is owed to Shelagh Kubish for her skillful editing, and to Nancy Foulds and Shane Kennedy for their encouragement.

To the "guardians of our past"—the numerous helpful individuals employed by the libraries, museums and historical societies of Texas—I am deeply indebted to you for sharing your expertise. Special thanks are owed to Sharon Van Dorn of the Dallas Public Library and Donna Woods of the Austin History Center, both of whom went above and beyond the call of duty to aid me. Other valuable research assistance was provided by the talented W. Ritchie Benedict of Calgary, Alberta, who can always be counted upon to deliver material that no one else would be able to find, and Andy Honigman, Associate Editor at *FATE* magazine. Andy went to extra effort on my behalf to find a number of articles and back issues containing Texas stories. *FATE* magazine itself deserves credit for being a priceless source of material. For many decades, it has served as a forum for people who wished to share and examine their paranormal experiences in a literary atmosphere that has always managed to be both open-minded and non-sensationalistic. Specific issues of *FATE* that were used as reference material but not mentioned within the text include April and November 1969; February, June and November 1970; July 1971; May and September 1972; March, August and October 1973; November 1974; November 1998; April and May 1999; and July, August and October 2000.

While speaking of source material, I would like to make grateful mention of the many talented individuals who have gone before me in this field. Those journalists, paranormal investigators and folklorists, often local experts, significantly enriched my experience as an author. I salute you and thank you.

Finally, I need to publicly thank the people whom I treasure in my private life. My mother-in-law, Stella, is so very generous with her time whenever we need a little extra help on the home front. My dear friend and fellow author, Barbara Smith, helps me in ways both tangible and intangible with every project that I do. And for my sweet-hearts—my husband, Dennis, and our children, Steven, Gracie, William and Natalie—I reserve my greatest gratitude and love. I do it all for you, and could not do it without you. Amen.

Introduction

When you say "Texas," people think "big." And no wonder: this is a state of outsized myths and vast spaces, a state encompassing so many regions and cultures, it could be—and once was—its own country. With its Wild West spirit, geographical diversity, dramatic history and sheer size, I felt certain that Texas would have a wealth of ghost stories. What do you know—for once in my life, I was right. Texans love to tell tales that start with the words "It was a dark and stormy night ... "

There are reasons this introductory line is a favorite among tellers of ghost stories. Within the space of a few words, it conjures up drama, dread and mystery. We all love to be frightened—it satisfies some deep-seated need—and one of the things that frightens us is the unknown. Ghost stories are rife with mystery, but inexplicable phenomena are not their only attraction. When we read these stories, we are also reassured by the possibility that our spirits are eternal. From a literary perspective, ghost stories really are terrifically efficient. They manage to push all of our buttons at once.

The ghost story is an age-old genre that has recently been rejuvenated by an increasing interest in the question of whether or not ghosts actually exist. More and more people seem determined to study ghosts in a scientific fashion. Investigative organizations are springing up around the country and around the world, and a body of knowledge is slowly but surely accumulating.

Given the masses of folklore and growing scientific knowledge, can it be said that anyone truly understands ghosts? The answer would still seem to be "No": ghosts vary so widely in nature, appearance and effect that no one definition can comprehend them all. Nevertheless, patterns of supernatural phenomena have led paranormal researchers to postulate different categories of hauntings.

There are spirits who are apparently intelligent and aware. They react to the circumstances and people around them.

There are other ghosts classed as "residual hauntings." They are less agents than imprints which someone has left upon his or her surroundings. For example, an old woman was accustomed to waking every night at 11 PM and walking down the stairs to the kitchen, where she would have tea and toast. For years after her death, the woman's family would hear her footsteps on the stairs every night at exactly 11 PM.

In many instances, specters continue about the business of their lives simply because they have not yet realized that they are dead. This often happens when death is sudden and unexpected. These phantoms become frustrated when they can't negotiate the physical landscape with their accustomed ease and are understandably upset when other people move into their homes, jobs and even marriages.

One thing is certain: whatever kind of ghost you're looking for, you will find an abundance of convincing examples in Texas. The state is rich with stories of the paranormal, ranging from the seriously investigated and convincing kind to engaging legends and folktales.

Because there are so many Texas ghost stories wanting to be told, it would be virtually impossible to produce a truly comprehensive collection. Instead, this book is what I believe to be a representative sampling of tales, including the famous, the never-before-told, the contemporary and the historical. (Some, I admit, made the cut simply because they are personal favorites.)

The question remains: are the stories true?

I believe that many are, and that most can be categorized as being true on some level. I'm a storyteller, however, not a paranormal investigator, and so will leave you to make those distinctions for yourself. I must add that the tales based on folklore rather than fact should not be dismissed. Their expression of the fears, superstitions and mores of a given time is just as valuable as the narration of a convincing supernatural event.

My sincere wish is that the following selections fulfill the traditional value of the ghost story. In other words, I hope that this book entertains you. Keep it close by, so that you can crack it open whenever you wish to be carried away to a mysterious place on a dark and stormy night.

These are the ghost stories of Texas. Enjoy!

Chapter 1

Historically Haunted

☠

Some of the most fascinating and believable ghost stories are those with historical roots. The intriguing blend of indisputable facts and elusive mysteries appeals to a wide audience. Those who ordinarily might not partake of paranormal fare find that archival records lend a satisfying layer of texture and substance to the ghost story. Similarly, people who find the usual historical texts just a little on the dry side are often drawn to the same information when a tantalizing tale of terror is woven in.

In Texas, there is plenty of material to please both the history buffs and the paranormal enthusiasts. So many dramatic events have taken place, and each one has left its own distinct mark—whether physical or psychic—on the Lone Star State.

The following are a few of the ghosts that make Texas so very historically haunted.

☠

The Driskill Hotel

It is near midnight, and there is a hush in the lushly appointed hallways of Austin's Driskill Hotel. Near the guest rooms of the top floor, an elevator door opens with a mechanical whisper and reveals that it carries no passengers. In the deserted hall, there is a movement of air, a suggestion of footsteps, a presence of personality, although no one can be seen. Then there is a pause, and the air appears to shimmer directly in front of one particular door. Moments later, inside the room, a woman is gently awakened by a gentle, flirtatious caress. In her state of twilight consciousness, it takes several seconds for her to realize that she is supposed to be alone ...

☠

Austin historian Mary Starr Barkley once said, "Probably no place in the Austin area is more heaped with history than the Driskill Hotel." There are likely none who would disagree with that. From the time of the magnificent hotel's opening to the present day, the Driskill has played an important part in all that has taken place in the state capital. In fact, the Driskill was significant from its moment of inception—it was to be Austin's first hotel, designed on a scale so grand and luxurious that it would draw guests from far and wide.

The man who held that original vision was a wealthy Texas cattle baron, Colonel Jesse Lincoln Driskill. In June 1884, Driskill chose a location and announced his plans to build. Two-and-a-half years later, those plans finally

The Driskill Hotel, 1894

came to fruition, and the impressive $400,000 hotel opened to tremendous fanfare.

Three days prior to the grand opening, the *Daily Statesman* of December 17, 1886, promised its readers "an accurate description of one of the finest hotels in the whole country." It then went on to expound upon the virtues of the Driskill, employing adjectives as ornate as the architecture.

There was no doubt that the majestic brick and limestone building was impressive enough to inspire such florid language. High stone arches, elaborate carvings and splendid marble columns gave it substance and importance. The finest materials and craftsmanship made it luxurious and plush. The appointments were first class, and the technology—including a hydraulic elevator and a bell system that enabled guests to ring for assistance from the comfort of their rooms—was the most advanced of the day. *The Daily Statesman* called the Driskill "this palace hotel of the south," and all who saw it agreed.

Colonel Driskill must have been proud to give his name to such a resplendent structure. It's a good thing that he did, for while his name remained, literally carved in stone, the man himself did not. Within one year of the spectacular opening, the financially strapped Colonel was forced to close his proud monument. It was the first of countless changes in ownership of the hotel. The Driskill saw three different proprietors within its first four years alone, and there would be many more to come.

Though the Driskill was known for changing hands, it was nevertheless better known as the scene of many significant events in Austin's history. It was the first hotel south and west of St. Louis to feature electric lighting. In October 1898, Austin's first long-distance telephone call was placed from the lobby of the Driskill. It is even rumored that when the Texas Rangers formed the plan that would eventually stop the legendary bank robbers Bonnie and Clyde, they did so in a suite at the Driskill Hotel. These events alone would have secured a page in history for the hotel, yet they pale in comparison to the Driskill's impact in the state's political arena.

The Driskill was once perfectly described by author and history professor Joe B. Frantz as the "living room for Texas politics." Writer David Hanners agreed; in his December 21, 1986, *Dallas Morning News* article concerning the hotel's centennial celebration, he wrote,

[T]he Driskill has presided over the financial and political fortunes of those who would be king and those who would be dethroned. Its rooms have played host to nervous politicians—Lyndon Johnson chief among them—who have sweated out election returns into the wee hours. Its ballrooms have been the scene of elegant inaugural balls of many of the state's governors. Its bar has long been the haunt of lobbyists eager to bend a legislator's ear over a stiff drink.

Past statesmen seemed to agree. According to former Governor Price Daniel, "If you were interested in Texas government, the Driskill is where you hung out." Indeed, it was once said that if you wanted to find anyone who amounted to anything, you looked first in the Driskill lobby, and then its bar.

Being the scene of such influence made the Driskill important, not only to Austinites, but to all Texans. In his 1973 book *The Driskill,* Joe B. Frantz wrote, "To the sensitive Texan there could be no peace in Valhalla unless he had spent at least one night within the Driskill before committing his body to the Lord." Frantz might have added that, for some, the Driskill held such tremendous appeal that they were choosing to stay on even after "committing" their bodies elsewhere. Somewhere along the line, people began to say that one of the most haunted buildings in Austin was the Driskill Hotel.

Over the years, stories accumulated about employees and guests who had never checked out of the Driskill. The housekeepers spoke of hearing footsteps behind them in the halls yet finding no one there when they turned to greet the person. The office telephones were known to act in strange ways. Some guests complained that their luggage was moved around their room at night as they slept. Of course, no hotel employee would have entered the room, and no rational explanation could ever be found.

The paranormal explanation that many offered, over the years, was that the haunting was connected to two tragic events that had taken place at the Driskill. According to legend, a murder had been committed in one room and a suicide in another. Those unhappy spirits were said to be trapped at the Driskill. But they were not alone.

This prestigious hotel seems to be the afterlife abode of several ghosts. One who resides on the fifth floor— an African-American night watchman with a pocket watch—was known in life to be a faithful employee of the Driskill. After working at the hotel for more than 20 years, the gentleman retired and then passed away. For decades following his death, hotel guests would inquire about the fellow with the pocket watch who was manning the desk on the fifth floor.

In 1998, the Driskill's banquet manager, Arthur Cicchese, related an incredible supernatural experience he had at the hotel one early morning as he prepared to open the restaurant.

"Outside the restaurant, there's a double set of elevators," Cicchese explained, "and there's this mirror that covers the whole area in front of the elevators." Cicchese was standing directly in front of that mirror between the elevators, adjusting his tie, at just before six o'clock one morning.

"Both elevators started to swoop down," he said. "I could hear laughter getting louder and louder." When the elevator stopped at his level, Cicchese expected to see a group of late-night revelers spill out into the hall. Instead, both elevator doors opened simultaneously, revealing that they were absolutely empty. What startled Cicchese at that point was that the sound of laughter had grown even louder.

"I'm still looking in the mirror," Cicchese explained. "I see nothing behind me. Laughter is now several people; very loud. I feel this cold breeze behind my neck; [it gave me] goose bumps all over. I turn around and, as I turn around, I still see nothing. But the laughter got even louder, as the spirits seemed to say, 'Look, he turned around to find us!'" As Arthur Cicchese realized that he had just been the object of spectral ridicule, the sound of the phantom merrymakers trailed off in the direction of the hotel's lobby.

"Now, it was a good experience," Cicchese later recalled. "I didn't feel spooked or scared. I felt like, well, these were definitely several spirits that had been partying all night, and here it was—five thirty, quarter to six in the morning—[and they still] sounded like they were inebriated." Although it was Cicchese's first personal experience with the Driskill's paranormal side, he added that there were "a million other ghost stories floating around the hotel."

One Driskill ghost has even managed to become somewhat famous, immortalized in the 1992 single "Ghost of a Texas Ladies' Man" by a band named Concrete Blonde. The band's lead singer, Johnette Napolitano, wrote the song after having her own strange encounter while staying at the Driskill.

In the April/May 1992 issue of *Network*, Napolitano recounted her experience. "The TV would work, and then it wouldn't," she said. "My key fit in the lock, and then it didn't .... I went to bed that night, turned the light off and closed my eyes, and the light went back on."

Napolitano explained that the light was so persistent in turning itself on that she eventually resorted to unplugging the lamp. The ghost, however, would not be that easily discouraged. As Napolitano lay there in the dark, she suddenly heard a creaking sound. "I opened my eyes and the light was on in the closet and the door was creaking open, just like someone was opening it slowly," she said.

The singer was frightened but didn't let her fear get the better of her. She spoke calmly to the ghost, saying, "I know you're here and I know you won't hurt me," then somehow managed to go to sleep.

In the light of day, Napolitano may have wondered if her imagination had been playing a trick on her. She was assured otherwise when talking to a drummer who was traveling on the same tour. He told her stories about a phantom on the fifth floor of the hotel that was known for making amorous advances toward female guests. "It only goes for single women," Napolitano concluded.

As fascinating as the hotel's supernatural activity is, it's just as amazing that the Driskill Hotel and its resident spirits are still in Austin. By 1970, despite the building's designation as a State Historic Landmark and its inclusion in the National Register of Historic Places, the wrecking ball was a real threat. The fading grande dame was about to be torn down and replaced by a parking lot when fate, in the form of a citizens' group led by the Austin Heritage Society, stepped in. The group raised enough money to stop the demolition and renovate the building. It reopened in 1973, in true Driskill fashion, with a gala ball.

Since then, the hotel has gone through several periods of extensive refurbishing and renovation. That care and attention has made the Driskill once again the magnificent and historic heart of the capital. Now in its second century, it manages to graciously showcase its past while offering every possible comfort and convenience of the modern age.

If, on occasion, that past intrudes a bit on the present-day landscape with a sudden chill or a shifting shadow that suggests an unexpected visitor from days gone by, most people are understanding and even welcoming. After all, over the decades, the Driskill set the scene for countless dramas and even starred in a few. It is understandable that some ghosts have chosen to return to such an emotionally and energetically charged location.

Arthur Cicchese summed it up well in 1998 when he said, "The building is 112 years old, you should expect that there are some spirits floating around," then added his personal assessment, "I think they're all friendly."

A glorious Texas hotel, populated by agreeable ghosts: that's the Driskill, embodying the true "spirit" of southern hospitality.

(Port) Arthur Stilwell

Anyone who doubts that the spirit world can accomplish great things will find proof to the contrary in the city of Port Arthur, Texas. This community owes its very existence to a legion of disembodied voices that counseled its namesake, railroad tycoon Arthur Stilwell.

Stilwell was a 15-year-old farm boy in Indiana when he first realized his strange gift. One evening he sat alone in his room, doing schoolwork by the flickering light of a coal oil lamp. He was having trouble concentrating on his lessons as the image of a lovely young neighbor girl intruded persistently on his thoughts. The teenaged Stilwell had become nearly hopelessly lost in reverie when he was startled away from his romantic fantasies by a strange, echoing voice. It told the young man not to waste time worrying about that particular girl and added, "You will not marry for four years hence and your bride will be Genevieve Wood."

The voice proved to be correct. Four years later, Arthur Stilwell married Genevieve Wood and told her about the voices which, since that night, had spoken to him on a regular basis. Although Stilwell had fast learned not to share this information with too many people—certain classmates and teachers had been quick to brand him a lunatic—he paid close attention to what the voices said and allowed them to guide his life. He assured his young wife that the spirits who advised him had his best interests at heart. Stilwell's bride must have believed him because, right after their wedding, the newlyweds packed their few things and moved to Kansas City, at the suggestion of the invisible guides.

Stilwell took a job as a clerk in a Kansas City brokerage house. He found the work agreeable and learned a great deal about finance as he watched fortunes rise and fall in the markets. One day, while tidying his desk at the end of a busy afternoon, Arthur Stilwell heard from his spirit advisors again. The voices told him to start his own railroad. It seemed an absurd request to make of a clerk who earned no more than $40 in a week, but Stilwell had long before learned to trust his voices. Besides, they assured him that the necessary funds would be easily obtained.

Again, the prediction was correct. Within a year, Stilwell had earned enough on the investor's market to launch the Kansas City Belt Line Railroad. He was in business, and his invisible guides remained with him. Between their savvy suggestions and Stilwell's hard work, the line quickly became one of the most profitable in the country.

Once both the Kansas City Belt Line and Arthur Stilwell's fortune had been well established, the invisible voices instructed that it was time to begin another railway project. This time, the spirits intoned, the tracks should stretch from Kansas City to the Gulf of Mexico. Stilwell listened to his guides, as always, and planned another railroad. The terminus was to be in Galveston, Texas. That plan remained in place until the project was nearly complete. Then the voices revisited Stilwell and expressed a sudden change of heart.

"Change direction," they warned. "If the railroad goes to Galveston, it will be doomed. Instead, go toward the swamps."

Arthur Stilwell endured the wrath of his investors and listened, as always, to his spirits. It was a seemingly insane change of plan, but Stilwell purchased a huge tract of inexpensive swampland on the north shore of Sabine Lake and made it the southern terminus of his new railroad. There were many at the time who dismissed Stilwell as an irrational fool who was about to be parted from his millions. Those same naysayers quickly changed their minds, however, when the devastating hurricane of 1900 virtually leveled Galveston. Stilwell's swampland terminus—by then a thriving seaport—remained unscathed. Better than unscathed, in fact, for the Kansas City Southern line earned a tidy sum by arranging the transport of relief supplies to the storm-battered citizens of Galveston.

For all his days, Arthur Stilwell heeded the advice of the spirit voices and, in return, they always served him well. With the help of his paranormal guides, Stilwell built seven railroads, wrote 30 books, amassed a fortune of $160 million and founded more than 40 towns. Of those, two bear his name. They are Stilwell, Oklahoma, and that profitable piece of swampland where he chose to end the Kansas City Southern Railroad—Port Arthur, Texas.

Remembering the Alamo

It was the winter of 1836, and after a long period of steadily increasing hostilities, Texas was seeking its independence from Mexico. By late February, the Mexican army, led by General Antonio Lopez de Santa Anna, had reached San Antonio, forcing the vastly outnumbered Texan defenders to retreat within the walls of a fortified Franciscan mission. There, for 13 dramatic days, the small band of freedom fighters held out against 10 times their number. Finally, in the early morning hours of March 6, size and strength won out over courage. The mission fell, and its more than 180 defenders—including such famous names as David Crockett, William B. Travis, and James Bowie—died for the cause of liberty. Their valor would not be forgotten. Forever after etched into the minds of Texans, as a symbol of bravery and sacrifice, was the name of that mission: the Alamo.

The Alamo is one of the most famous historic sites in Texas, if not all of the United States. These four acres in the heart of San Antonio are visited by 2.5 million people every year. They come to learn the history, to pay respect to the memories of those who gave their lives and to witness the ghosts, for it seems that some essence of those brave defenders refuses to die.

The first supernatural tales regarding the Alamo came within weeks of the siege and were told by soldiers in the then-retreating Mexican army. Following Santa Anna's capture at the battle of San Jacinto, General Andrade ordered his troops southward. The small Mexican force occupying San Antonio was instructed to destroy the Alamo before

The Alamo—Texas's symbol of liberty

they departed. No symbol of the Texans' defiance was to be left behind. When the soldiers arrived to demolish the mission, however, they were greeted by entirely unexpected opposition. It seemed that the defenders of the Alamo were determined to continue defending it, even in death.

What actually happened is impossible to say. There are at least three popular versions of the story. In one, the soldiers were frightened away from their demolition task by ghostly hands protruding from the walls and brandishing lit torches. As the men cowered in fear, a hollow, spectral voice intoned, "Depart! Touch not these walls! He who desecrates these walls shall meet a horrible fate!" A second version of the legend has it that a party of men sent to blow up the chapel returned to their commander in a state of terror. Guarding the building, they said, were six spectral figures, diablos who held swords of fire. In the third tale, it is said that as Santa Anna's army prepared to leave the

city, the bodies of the Texan defenders were still smolder-
ing in several huge funeral pyres. As soldiers set out to
destroy the Alamo, a spirit rose from the flames of one
pyre and frightened the troops away.

All three legends agree on one point: the Mexican
forces were frightened away from their destruction of the
Alamo by some powerful supernatural force. Facts support the theory. An order was given to destroy the mission,
yet it was left standing. Today, the Defenders' Monument,
a marble cenotaph situated in front of the Alamo, depicts a
proud spirit rising from a pile of crumpled bodies.
Perhaps it's metaphorical, or perhaps it's paying respect
to the third version of the legend ...

Although the significance of the battle at the Alamo
was immediately understood and appreciated
("Remember the Alamo!" was Sam Houston's rousing cry
during the battle of San Jacinto), the building itself did not
immediately become a revered shrine of Texas liberty.
During the late 1800s, it served other purposes for various tenants, including the U.S. government, the
Confederate army, and the San Antonio Police
Department. During that time, the Alamo also became a
location of great interest to those who were curious about
ghost stories—for according to many, many witnesses, the
old mission was haunted.

There were reports of a ghostly sentry, whose even
footsteps could be heard crossing the south side of the roof,
from east to west, on cold, rainy nights. On the hottest,
sunniest of days, a man was often seen walking around the
property in a rain-soaked, full-length riding coat, water
dripping off the brim of his hat. Those who believed this

apparition to be a spirit of the Alamo were quick to remind people that the siege took place during heavy rains.

In 1871, one of the most dramatic paranormal events to ever be witnessed at the Alamo took place. The night before the city of San Antonio was to dismantle part of the original mission, guests at the neighboring Menger Hotel were stunned as they watched ghostly figures marching along the walls that were slated to come down. The spectral protest was witnessed by a number of people, and no rational explanation could be found.

In February 1894, the *San Antonio Express News* ran an article concerning "the rumors of the manifestations of alleged ghosts who are said to be holding bivouac around that place so sacred to the memory of Texas's historic dead." The article told of "a new feature of the case," a 14-year-old medium who had visited the building (then police quarters) and offered the police captain, Jacob Coy, an opportunity to communicate with the spirits.

Captain Coy asked the spirits who they were, and the response came, "the defenders of the Alamo." That came as no surprise. When he asked the entities to explain their purpose, however, the answer was unexpected. The young medium said, "They say that there is buried in the walls of the building $540,000 in $20 gold pieces. They also say that they are anxious to have the money discovered and have been waiting for a chance to communicate with the people on earth about it and have it discovered. They will relinquish all claim to the treasure in favor of the person who finds it." Unfortunately, the young medium snapped out of her trance before the spirits were able to get too specific about the actual location of the gold.

It was not the first talk of buried treasure beneath the Alamo. There had long been stories that in the month prior to the onslaught the defenders had packed all of their valuables into one of the mission bells. The bell was then buried, as a means of keeping the men's personal wealth safe during what was certain to be a tumultuous time. Some theorize that the ghostly guardians have since been keeping a jealous watch over this cache. While anything is possible, that hardly seems consistent with the spirit of selfless heroism that the Alamo represents.

Today, visitors to the historic site still talk of ghosts. The rain-soaked apparition in the Alamo garden is regularly seen, and there have been many modern accounts of a spirit who paces frantically back and forth atop the mission walls. Other, more subjective, reports tell of unexplainable cold spots within the buildings, as well as a pervasive feeling of sadness. One has to wonder if the sadness actually lives within the Alamo or is projected by visitors to the shrine. Certainly, this is the type of memorial where people leave as much emotional energy as they take away.

Perhaps that exchange of energy serves to recharge a psychic battery of sorts. Perhaps the spirits of the Texas defenders remain simply because they were denied a proper burial. Or perhaps, because of the sudden and violent nature of their deaths, these heroes simply have yet to recognize that they have passed on.

Ultimately, the reason for the haunting is irrelevant. All that matters in the end is that the true spirit of the Alamo—both literally and figuratively speaking—lives on.

☠

The Alamo has been described as San Antonio's "supernatural epicenter." As such, it seems to be affecting its closest neighbors in a decidedly paranormal fashion. The 150-year-old Menger Hotel, overlooking the Alamo, is becoming as famous for its phantoms as it is for its historical elegance. Not only do guests enjoy a perfect view of spectral activities at the old mission, but they are highly likely to encounter one of the hotel's own apparitions. Among the many that have been reported are a frontiersman who floats a few feet above the floor and chats with an invisible companion; a Civil War soldier who beckons to people in the bar; and a chambermaid who stands in the hallway folding towels, although she was murdered by her husband a century ago. The current total of guests and employees who have never checked out of the Menger is said to be a whopping 34.

The Hanging of Chipita Rodriguez

On the banks of the Nueces River, near the little town of San Patricio, Texas, a shadow moves in the moonlight. A soft sound is carried on the wind. It is a mournful sigh, then a gentle sobbing that can be heard above the soothing sound of the river. Suddenly, a dark shape can be seen: the silhouette of a woman gliding along a path near the water. At the base of an old mesquite tree, the figure pauses. Her head tilts slightly back, and she emits an unearthly wail. The cry pierces the night air, freezing the blood of any who hear it. It is the lament of Chipita Rodriguez, who suffers eternally for in injustice committed nearly a century and a half ago.

☠

In 1998, as convicted murderer Karla Faye Tucker sat awaiting her death by lethal injection, Texans were haunted by both the ghost and the memory of the last woman to be executed by the state: Chipita Rodriguez. Although there were 134 years between the two events, comparisons were inevitable. Time and time again, both the facts and the legend surrounding Rodriguez's hanging were recounted in the media, and her memory was evoked repeatedly by Tucker's supporters. Gender aside, the cases were dissimilar, though, particularly as Tucker had admitted her guilt and Rodriguez had always maintained her innocence.

In 1963, 100 years after the woman's death, state legislators agreed with Rodriguez's declaration of innocence and voted for a resolution stating that she did not receive a fair trial. By that time, Chipita had been staging her own effective protest by haunting the banks of the Nueces for a century.

"No soy culpable"—"I am not guilty"—was all Chipita ever said at her own trial for murder. Certainly, the evidence against her was never more than circumstantial. A view of the facts today suggests that the poor woman may have simply been in the wrong place at the wrong time.

During the years of the Civil War, Chipita Rodriguez was an innkeeper, running a place near San Patricio that was popular with gamblers and cowboys alike. The business may have been a little rough, but Chipita knew how to handle herself and managed to make a decent living.

In 1863, a horse trader named John Savage rode up to Chipita's inn, seeking a meal and a night's lodgings. He had with him some heavily packed saddlebags, as he was carrying hundreds of pieces of gold. Later, the jury at Chipita's trial would be asked to believe that Chipita had her eyes fixed greedily upon those riches. Whether she did or not can never be known for sure. What is known is that Savage's body was later found stuffed into some gunny sacks. He had been hacked to death with the axe that Chipita used to split her kindling.

Chipita Rodriguez was charged with murder and found guilty. The prosecution said that the motive had been robbery, even though the gold-filled saddlebags were found near Savage's body. That, and the fact that Chipita refused to speak in her own defense, made many

San Patricio residents believe that the innkeeper was protecting someone. County historian Keith Guthrie once told the *Corpus Christi Caller-Times*, "People said it was an illegitimate son who actually did the axe work."

Even the jury appeared doubtful. Although they returned a guilty verdict, the members of the jury recommended leniency for Chipita Rodriguez. The judge, however, would have none of it. He ordered that at sunset on Friday, November 13, 1863, Chipita was to be "hanged by the neck until dead."

The sentence was carried out by the river, the only location with a suitably high tree. Then, when Chipita was dead, her swinging corpse was cut down and buried on the spot. In February 1998, San Patricio Mayor Lonnie Glasscock III told the *Caller-Times* that burying the body by the river "was apparently a big no-no. People say her soul will forever be in limbo because she wasn't buried in the cemetery."

Perhaps Chipita is protesting her improper burial, or perhaps she is protesting her innocence. For whatever reason, she has been seen frequently over the years, drifting by the trees along the Nueces, issuing her sorrowful cry. It seems that she is determined to never be forgotten.

Toward that end, the woman's spirit has been successful in pervading popular culture. Books, articles, at least one epic poem and even an opera have been written about Chipita Rodriguez and serve to keep her memory etched in the collective consciousness of all Texans. Her life and death have been studied by thousands, and she has carved out a place in history that she could never have achieved by living her life out fully as a simple innkeeper. One has to wonder, does Chipita know? And does this provide her with some small consolation?

It seems unlikely to those who pass the Nueces late at night and bear witness to that woeful cry.

☠

Chipita Rodriguez's execution is not the only hanging to haunt Texas. In 1921, Albert Howard was hanged in the south Texas town of Gonzales. He spent the weeks leading up to his execution protesting his innocence and staring through his jail-cell window at the courthouse clock as it counted down the remaining hours of his life. By the time Howard was led away to the gallows, he was nearly insane. He shook his fists and screamed at the clock tower, swearing that it would never tell another man when he was about to die.

From that day forward, the clock never worked properly. Despite many attempts to repair it, the four separate faces always showed different times, none of them correct. Albert Howard's claim of innocence is a matter for debate, but there is no doubt that he is able to lay an effective curse.

Ghostly Goliad

One of the terrible tragedies that took place during Texas's battle for independence was the horrific massacre of those stationed at the Presidio of La Bahia at Goliad. Colonel James Walker Fannin and 352 of his men had been captured by Mexican General Santa Anna's forces at the Battle of Coleto. One week later, on March 27, 1836, every one of those soldiers was executed. Today, the historic fortress seems to bear the psychic scars of that dreadful time.

Several years ago, a security guard who was assigned to a special duty at the Presidio spent a strange and terrifying night enduring a variety of ghostly experiences. The guard was accustomed to working at night, was not prone to flights of fancy and began his shift fully expecting an uneventful few hours. According to the November 8, 1992, *Victoria Advocate*, the man's expectations changed just before midnight when the silence was broken by an eerie chorus of wailing infants.

The guard was shaken by the hollow, unearthly quality of the cries. He would later say that they were the cries of "pain and suffering." Despite his fear, the guard did his duty and tried to track the frightening sound to its source. It wasn't easy to do, but he eventually realized that the crying was emanating from a number of unmarked graves near the chapel.

At some point, the piercing howls came to an abrupt end. The guard had barely begun to register his relief when the chilling voices of a women's choir filled the air. The lyrics and tune were unrecognizable, and the song seemed to come from within a wall of the fortress. The effect was haunting, but not nearly as frightening as what was to come.

Before the night ended, the nervous guard had also been visited by two separate apparitions: a small, barefoot friar clad in a black robe, and a woman in a flowing, white dress.

The friar seemed to form out of a cloud of vapor that arose from the ground in front of the chapel. He was no more than four feet tall, and his face was obscured by the hood of his robe. The ghost seemed oblivious to the security guard's presence as he wandered around the church muttering prayers in Latin. Eventually, his religious duty done, the little fellow vanished.

Ninety minutes after the strange friar's disappearance, the guard saw another spirit materialize in front of his eyes. It was the woman in white, and she appeared in front of one of the unmarked graves from which the earlier crying sounds had come. She appeared to be searching for something. Suddenly, in a moment that must have been filled with sheer terror for the guard, the specter turned around and looked directly at him. Their eyes met, then the wraith levitated and began to float toward the rear wall. The spirit continued to drift, over the wall and off in the direction of an aged cemetery.

What the hapless security guard experienced on that eerie night might have easily been dismissed if not for one thing: many people had reported having nearly identical experiences at the old fort. There were others who had heard the wailing infants and the ghostly female chorus. There were others who had seen the phantom friar. The guard was not alone in witnessing anything and, in fact, had actually missed out on a number of haunting events that were known to occur regularly at the Presidio.

Regular employees of the fort were accustomed to seeing lights appear in the chapel, very late at night. They were also used to feeling uneasy and to being enveloped by unusually cold pockets of air. There were many spooky tales told by those who worked within the Presidio, but perhaps the most chilling story of all came from those who simply lived in the area.

According to a 1984 Halloween article in the *Texan Express*, drivers alone in their vehicles late at night, passing over the San Antonio River, would sometimes experience the fright of a lifetime. Some movement, detected out of the corners of their eyes, would cause them to glance to their right. There, they would suddenly discover someone sitting in their passenger seat. At second glance, the person would be gone, but not before nearly causing the driver to lose control of the vehicle owing to sheer terror.

One has to assume it's just another ghostly resident of the Presidio, trying to hitch a ride away from this sad place of unhappily trapped souls.

The Ghostly Governor's Mansion

It would be the most famous house in Texas even if it did not have a ghost. But the Governor's Mansion, on Colorado Avenue in Austin, is haunted by not just one, but two spirits. There is the tortured soul of a young man, and the apparition of one of the state's most revered heroes, both of whom suffered great disappointments, died during the Civil War years and chose this stately home as their afterlife residence. Aside from those similarities, these two phantoms have little in common.

There aren't many Texas schoolchildren who couldn't tell you something about Sam Houston. Houston was the first president of the transient Republic of Texas and the seventh governor of the state. He was undeniably a great man, yet Houston was unceremoniously ousted from his official residence and ejected from office when he refused to pledge his allegiance to the Confederacy as the Civil War approached. The humiliation of leaving the mansion under such circumstances must have been almost too much for the venerated father of Texas to bear. He died only a few years later—disgraced, brokenhearted and perhaps worrying that his ejection from office would overshadow his long and otherwise glorious list of accomplishments. Those thoughts must have haunted him in his final years, so it is little wonder that Sam Houston returned to haunt the scene of his dishonor. It was not long after his death that visitors to the

The Governor's Mansion had already been haunted for nearly a quarter century when this photo was taken in 1888.

Governor's Mansion began to report fleeting glimpses of the old man, a stooped, sad-eyed figure that would vanish whenever someone tried to approach it.

Over the decades, Houston has proved to be as steadfast in death as he was in life. His somber presence has been felt by numerous governors and their families, who have claimed that the specter rattles dishes and windows and stomps through the mansion in his boots.

In the mid-1980s, Governor Mark White's daughter Elizabeth refused to enter the bedroom directly opposite that of her parents, saying that something about it frightened her. That "something" might have been the ghost of Sam Houston, for that room had been his bedroom when he was in residence. First Lady Gale White understood her daughter's feelings, for she had had an encounter of her own with the late general.

One evening, as Gale White prepared to retire, she noticed that, in Sam Houston's former bedroom, a light had been left shining over his portrait. Mrs. White stepped into the room and extinguished the lamp, then closed the door behind her and went across the hall to bed.

The next morning, Mrs. White was the first person in the mansion to rise. When she walked out of her bedroom, she was surprised to see that the door across the hall was wide open, and the lamp was once again shining on the portrait. The First Lady felt that Sam Houston's spirit may have been responsible for the strange event. "Sam must be walking these halls," she told a reporter, "and he's not even supposed to be the ghost here."

The fellow who "is supposed to be the ghost," to borrow Gale White's phrase, is not famous by name. He is best known by his family connections, as he was the 19-year-old nephew of Pendleton Murrah, governor of Texas during the Civil War. The boy had been visiting Murrah in the Governor's Mansion in 1864 when his romance with a lovely young woman turned sour.

The story goes that the girl had been flirtatious and encouraging until her suitor proposed marriage. She then turned cold and rejected the poor fellow. Heartsick and utterly crestfallen, the boy locked himself in the north bedroom of the mansion. At precisely midnight, he put a pistol to his head and pulled the trigger. He had obviously planned to put an end to his suffering but, within days of the boy's tragic end, people were beginning to suspect that he had not been entirely successful.

Pained moans and wails could be heard coming from the bedroom, and the air within it had suddenly become extremely cold. If Governor Murrah was aware of the room's sudden change of atmosphere, it is unlikely that he devoted much thought to it. With the South rapidly losing the war and Murrah losing his own personal battle with tuberculosis, other concerns occupied his mind. In fact, only a short time after his nephew's suicide, Texas surrendered to Union forces, and the governor was forced to flee to Mexico. He left many unfinished bits of personal business behind—including his wife, who had to be taken in by relatives, and the nasty job of cleaning up the mess in the north bedroom.

Servants who had been left to take care of the mansion were not about to mop up the gore. They were already refusing to enter the haunted room. It wasn't long before the help was fleeing the mansion just as the governor had done. It wasn't the Yankees striking fear into their hearts, however. It was the ghost.

The blood-spattered wall was still waiting when the Union-appointed governor, Andrew Hamilton, moved into the mansion. The horrid mess was finally cleaned, but there was little that the maids could do about the tortured ghost. Day in and day out, the specter of the boy wailed and cried in anguish. Sometimes there were noises of banging on the walls of the room. On Sundays, the day when he had pulled the trigger, the sobbing grew worse. Finally, the spirit became as much an embarrassment as a fright to the new governor, and he ordered the room to be sealed. When it was reopened, years later, the sounds of despair could still be heard. They serve as a sad reminder of the tragedy and are said to persist to this day.

Chapter 2

"It Happened to Me..."

While witnessing the paranormal is not prerequisite to believing in it, there is still nothing quite so convincing as a personal experience. Even the most steadfast skeptics are easily converted when faced with a misty apparition, an unexplainable event or a profound psychic insight. As for those who already believe, an encounter with the strange and mysterious only serves to strengthen their conviction.

This absolute assurance—coupled with the fact that the details have not been filtered through numerous sources— means that people who have had their own experiences with paranormal phenomena tell some of the best stories. After all, a firsthand account from a true believer ranks as extremely credible when compared to a legend that has been passed from person to person, or even generation to generation.

The following tales come from a number of Texans who can honestly say, "It happened to me ... "

A Whispered Warning

It was a lovely May evening in 1967, and Charles and Sandra Ray had just finished dinner. They were relaxed as they exchanged stories of the day. Increasingly, however, Sandra found it difficult to concentrate on the conversation. For no apparent reason she was becoming anxious, and her mind kept drifting to thoughts of her younger brother, Joe, a university student in New Orleans.

Joe was planning to drive home to Dallas for a visit that week. Charles Ray suggested to his wife that she was simply nervous about her brother's being on the highway and assured her that the drive was easy and nothing to be concerned about. Still, Sandra fretted throughout the evening and by bedtime felt much too tense to sleep. Sandra had no way of reaching her brother, so she called her parents.

"Is anything wrong, Mom? I just can't shake this feeling."

Sandra's mother assured her that all was well in their home, but Sandra's anxiety continued to grow, and she spent the entire night pacing the floor and worrying about her brother. Early the next morning, the phone rang. When Sandra picked up the receiver and heard Joe's voice, she nearly fainted with relief. And when he told her what had happened to him the previous evening, she finally understood her strange foreboding.

Joe had set out driving the night before, but his car battery died before he even left the New Orleans city limits. When he pulled over to the curb, the car behind him pulled over as well. Two men got out and walked toward Joe. They were shadowy figures, silhouetted in the headlights of their own vehicle.

"Do you need some help, there?" one of them called, as they approached. "Can we lend a hand?"

They sounded like good Samaritans, but Joe later told Sandra that he knew instantly that something was amiss. He was right. It soon became apparent that the men intended to rob him, not help him. A gun was drawn, a fight ensued, and Joe was luckily able to fend off his attackers and get back into his car. He prayed for a miracle as he turned the ignition key, and his prayer was answered when the dead engine roared to life. Joe sped off and drove to the nearest filling station, where he regained his composure and purchased a brand new battery.

"I took a bit of a beating, but I'm thankful I wasn't murdered," he finished.

Sandra was stunned. "How did you know, Joe?" she asked. "You said you knew right away that there was going to be trouble, but how did you know?"

There was a brief silence on the line. Then Joe answered. "You tell me, Sis," he said, "because when those men first approached me, it was your voice I heard, whispering in my ear."

"You said, 'Danger, my brother, danger!'"

Midget

In the 1950s, a couple named Bill and Barbara ran the Kozy Kourt Motel in Electra, Texas. They had an assistant who was never on the payroll: Barbara's little dog, Midget, whom she had raised from a puppy. If someone drove up to the motel's office while Bill and Barbara were busy in one of the other cabins, Midget would alert them by barking. Because the couple handled everything from housekeeping chores to repair jobs, Midget's habit of announcing potential guests was very useful. No matter what Bill and Barbara were busy with, they never missed a customer.

In March 1951, Bill took a few days off to go fishing, knowing the Kozy Kourt would be well cared for by his wife and her small, furry assistant. While he was gone, however, Midget became very ill. By the time Barbara could get her beloved pet to a veterinarian, it was too late to save him. The doctor told her that Midget was suffering terribly from an advanced case of blood poisoning. On March 15, the little animal was mercifully put to sleep.

Exactly one month later, Barbara was cleaning one of the motel cabins when she heard a familiar barking. *That's Midget!* she thought, although she knew it could not be. Nevertheless, when the barking persisted, she decided to walk over to the office and look around. The noise stopped as soon as Barbara entered the office. There she found customers waiting to rent out two of her cabins.

The next day, Barbara left the quiet motel unattended and went down the street to have dinner with a friend.

Just as she started her meal, she heard Midget's recognizable bark. This time, Barbara didn't hesitate. She rushed back down the block and caught a carful of people just as they were pulling out of the lot. That night, thanks to her departed pooch, Barbara rented out every single cabin in the motel.

Two days after that, Barbara was cleaning a cabin when she again heard Midget announcing a customer. When she looked across to the office, however, she saw no vehicle, so she went back to her work. When the frantic barking continued for several minutes, Barbara decided it would be best to go over to the office, if only to silence her spectral pet. When she walked in, she found a man waiting at the counter. "The door was not locked," he said, "and I knew you would come when you heard your dog barking." It was the third time, since his death, that Midget had saved the Kozy Kourt a bit of business.

In March 1952, exactly one year after Midget's passing, Barbara encountered the ghost of her little dog for the final time. She was working on the motel's books when she suddenly had a strange and powerful urge to walk to the front door of the office. Barbara had a great deal of work on her desk, so she tried to fight the impulse. In the end, however, she could not resist the mysterious feeling. She walked to the door, opened it, and looked outside. There, walking past the row of cabins, was Midget. The dog turned to look at Barbara for a few seconds, then simply faded away. She never saw him again, and she never again heard his helpful bark.

Jack's Cat

It was 1964—a warm August day in the small East Texas town of Killeen. Lois Selvidge was busy in the kitchen with her weekly baking. Sunshine streamed through the windows, illuminating the floury haze above the table where she kneaded and folded the sticky bread dough. Her work was interrupted when her four-year-old son, Jack, came bounding into the room.

"Can it sleep with me, Mommy?" The little boy's eyes were glittering with excitement, and he shifted impatiently from one foot to the other while he waited for Lois's answer.

The only problem was, she didn't know quite what he was asking.

"Can what sleep with you?"

"My cat," said Jack. The boy stared at his mother pleadingly.

"But you don't have a cat," she pointed out as she dropped another blob of dough into a well-buttered loaf pan. Lois's statement of the obvious did nothing to dampen Jack's enthusiasm.

"Daddy is bringing me one," he announced happily. "I saw him buy it."

Lois smiled at her son's imagination. Jack Sr. had been gone all day. Father and son had not seen each other since breakfast early that morning.

"Go on out and play in the yard," Lois said, as she gently shooed the little boy out of the kitchen. "If you keep pestering me with these crazy questions, I'll never get finished here."

Jack obediently played outdoors for the next two hours. Each time Lois glanced out the window to check on him, she chuckled to herself and thought that there was surely nothing more creative than the mind of a four-year-old boy.

At 5 PM, Lois's husband walked through the front door. "Where's Jack?" he asked, immediately. "I have a surprise for him."

"He's in the back yard," Lois said, then asked, "What kind of surprise?" Jack Sr. was carrying a small box under his arm, covered with an old cloth.

"Take a peek," he said. Lois lifted the cloth and saw something that made her catch her breath. There, curled in its cardboard nest, was a kitten. Gently, she stroked the animal's marmalade-colored fluff.

"Pretty, isn't she? Purebred. I know it was a bit of an impulse, but I took one look and figured Jackie would love her." The man beamed at the thought of showing the kitten to his son.

Lois looked up at her husband. "Where did you buy this kitten?" she asked.

"At the pet shop, in Temple." Temple was a good 20-mile drive from Killeen.

"What time?"

"About three o'clock."

It was the very time that young Jack announced that he had "seen" his father buying a kitten for him. At the time, Lois had marveled at the boy's imagination. A short two hours later, she was marveling at his apparent psychic abilities.

Jack Sr. grew concerned as he studied his wife's reaction.

"I know we didn't talk about this," he said, "but I didn't think it would be a problem."

"Oh, it's not," Lois assured him, as she ushered him toward the back door. "Go show Jackie his new kitten." As the screen door slammed shut behind her husband, Lois added to herself, "but he won't be as surprised as you think ... "

The Scary Airplane Movie

In 1969, Adam Manning (a pseudonym) was a three-year-old boy living with his parents in Uvalde, Texas. His mother, Doreen, says she will always remember a particular nightmare that Adam told her about on June 2 of that year.

The little boy had seemed tired and out of sorts when he arrived at the breakfast table that morning. Doreen was playful with him, but he remained moody. When Adam was asked what he wanted for breakfast, he claimed he wasn't hungry. Doreen asked him why.

"Because of the scary movie I saw last night," was the boy's reply.

Doreen was confused. She knew that Adam hadn't seen much television the day before, and what he had watched certainly hadn't been frightening. "What movie?" she asked, pressing him to be more specific.

"You know, the movie you watch when you go to sleep at night," Adam said.

Doreen understood then that her son had had a nightmare, and she suggested that he might feel better if he told her about it. He did just that—all the while shaking with fear as he recounted details so vivid and horrifying that Doreen couldn't believe they sprang from the imagination of such a young child.

His nightmare had been of an airline disaster. The plane crashed into a mountain, Adam said, and dead people were scattered all over the ground. Everyone who had been on the plane was killed. The people who saw the plane crash were Mexicans, and they lived in a place called "Monnaray."

"It was just a dream, and it's all over now," Doreen soothed her son. Secretly, she was alarmed that one could suffer such intense nightmares at the tender age of three.

Throughout the day, Doreen spoke to several friends and co-workers about Adam's "scary airplane movie." Finally, one woman who had listened carefully to the story asked, "Are you sure it was a dream? Maybe Adam's had a premonition."

It was something that Doreen had not considered. She thought the possibility was remote but still made a mental note to watch the papers for airline disasters in the months to come.

She had to wait only two days.

On June 4, 1969, Mexico recorded its most devastating airline accident to that date. A Mexicana Airlines Boeing 727 was descending when it crashed into the side of a mountain. All 79 people aboard were killed. The location? Just outside of Monterrey.

Or, as a toddler might say it, "Monnaray."

Speak Well of the Dead

In 1957, a Houston-area woman named Elaine suffered the loss of her dearest friend, Linda. Linda, along with her husband and one of their children, had died of asphyxiation in their Florida home. The tragedy was no doubt still weighing heavily on Elaine's mind several months later when Texas suffered an unusual cold spell and she found it necessary to turn on the gas heaters in her own apartment. The strange events that followed were documented in Hans Holzer's book, *Some of My Best Friends are Ghosts* (Manor Books, 1978).

Elaine and Linda had always shared their joys and cares, particularly where their children were concerned. Late that night, as her family slept, Elaine realized that from wherever she was, Linda continued to watch out for them.

It was two o'clock in the morning when Elaine awoke to the distinct impression that she had company. Before she fully opened her eyes, she heard her late friend's voice, as clearly as though the woman was in the room. "Elaine," Linda said, "get up and see about the boys."

The ominous message caused Elaine to snap to attention. She jumped out of bed and ran to her sons' bedroom. She found them sleeping peacefully but noticed that the flame on the heater had gone out, and the gas jet was wide open. Had she slept much longer, the result would have been tragic.

Elaine was trembling with relief as she turned off the gas. At that very moment, she was encircled by a cool mist.

Once again, she clearly heard Linda's voice. The specter laughed and said, "I told you."

Days later, Elaine was still upset by the experience. She was grateful for the life-saving warning but unnerved by the knowledge that she had a ghost in her midst. After several days of worry, she decided to call her minister for advice.

"Why would this woman's spirit still remain here?" he asked over the telephone. "What troubled her?"

Elaine had to admit that many things had troubled her friend. Linda had been a woman with many problems, and as Elaine sat alone in her living room, she freely revealed the many confidences that her late friend had once entrusted to her. As she spoke, she happened to glance at the gas heater.

Slowly, as though someone was turning it off, she saw the flame die out.

Elaine once again felt strongly that there was another presence in the room. This time, however, she sensed pure rage being directed at her and began to cry. Between terrified sobs, she choked out a few words telling the minister what was happening. "Leave the apartment!" he demanded. "Go now, Elaine!" But she couldn't move. Many minutes later, when the minister and his wife burst into the room, Elaine was still sitting in her living room, crying and clutching the telephone receiver.

Linda's spirit never visited Elaine again. Perhaps she had no reason to, or perhaps, as Elaine suspected, she was simply angry at being gossiped about, particularly after committing such a good deed. Nevertheless, Elaine would never again assume she was truly alone, and would always remember to speak well of the dead.

"I Was a Ghost!"

Mai Beaird of Denton, Texas, was only 15 years old when she experienced the most astounding event of her life. More than 50 years later, she would finally write about it: the time she returned from the other side of the grave.

It was the summer of 1917, and Mai had contracted what her family doctor described simply as "the fever." Her temperature rose until she was burning hot to the touch, and her head pounded in agony. On the third day of her illness, the doctor warned Mai's parents, "Nobody ever lives with this high a temperature." He was right. Within the hour, the physician could detect no pulse and declared Mai dead. What was incredible was that Mai would later recall seeing him do it.

Though her physical being had expired, the teenager realized that her spirit had been set free. As she watched her parents grieve over the wasted body in the bed, Mai marveled at her new form. She later recalled,

Now I could be wherever I chose to be. The walls of the room seemed to vanish. I was free, weightless, completely happy. And what energy! I'd never known such energy while I was encased in that body.

"That body," in fact, looked to Mai like a pain-filled prison from which she had escaped. It repelled her, and she rejoiced in her new expansive state. There was only one problem: Mai could not stand to see her beloved parents

The thought of spending eternity in a lonely and forgotten grave never concerned Mai Beaird, after her exhilarating near-death experience.

devastated by grief. She had to let them know she was alright.

Mai crossed the little bedroom and embraced her father. "I'm happy and free!" she told him. "I'll never be sick again!" But the man's hands never left his face. Mai spoke more loudly as she hugged her mother. "Can't you see me?" she implored. But the woman continued to weep uncontrollably. It was clear to Mai that she could never communicate with her mother and father as a free spirit, and she loved them too much to allow them to suffer. She would have to return to her body.

As Mai made her decision, two men arrived from the funeral home and lifted her corpse onto a stretcher. "At that instant," Mai wrote, "my love for my parents drew me back to my body like a rubber band snaps." She felt herself being carried down the hall and outside to the waiting hearse.

The energy and joy the girl had been filled with only moments before had vanished. Mai was back in a pain-wracked body, unable to move or even breathe. Paralyzed beneath the sheet, she was gripped suddenly by a new horror. *Oh, God!* Mai thought, *now I'm going to be buried alive!*

With tremendous effort, she managed to let one limp hand slide off the stretcher. One of the men noticed it, but simply balanced the stretcher on one knee while he tucked her arm back beneath the sheet. Again, Mai let her hand drop. Again, the young fellow placed it back where it belonged. With the last little bit of strength the girl could summon, she let her hand dangle off the stretcher one more time. This time the older, more experienced, mortician noticed.

"My God, she's still alive!" he screamed. The two shocked men dropped the stretcher on the floor. Mai's head hit the smooth, hard tile, and darkness descended.

For five days, Mai remained unconscious. When she awoke, she was surrounded by friends and family, and the doctor was monitoring her pulse. When Mai opened her eyes, the doctor placed a thermometer in her mouth. After a few moments, he read the results and spoke. "She has passed the crisis. She'll be alright with a few days' rest."

Mai felt well but was weak. In a whisper, she asked her father to have everyone else leave the room. Once they had, she told her father every detail of what had taken place in the room while she had been "dead." "Am I right?" she asked. "Is that the way everything happened?" The shocked man verified her story. Mai then explained to him that she knew these things because her disembodied spirit had been in the room the entire time. Her father was accepting but offered one piece of advice.

"For God's sake and your sake, don't ever tell anybody about it. No one will ever believe you."

Mai promised and, for more than half a century, kept that promise. Eventually, though, it was something she felt she had to share. She wanted others to know about this profound experience which, particularly in her senior years, had brought her a great measure of comfort.

"I really have no fear about what lies beyond the grave," she wrote. "After all, I've been there and back!"

A Spirit Brings Good News

In 1969, an Alpine, Texas, woman named Jane Giddens received one of the most welcome messages of her life—from a ghost.

It was a hot July afternoon, and Jane had hung the "closed" sign on the front door of her beauty salon early. She was tired and wanted to go home for a nap. Jane needed to rest her body, and her mind, which had been consumed with worry about her son Butch, a sergeant with the 196th Light Infantry Division in Vietnam.

Butch's wife had given birth to their first child, a daughter named Jamie Lynn, only weeks before. Still, he was not scheduled to return home until October. The fighting was particularly bad and, in his letters, it became increasingly clear that Butch was beginning to doubt that he would make it back to his family. As Jane lay down on the couch to rest on that July day, she was wishing that there was some way he could come home sooner.

As Jane slept, she began to dream that there was a party taking place in the house. Many people milled about, laughing and talking. None of them seemed to notice when the front door opened and a young man in army combat clothes walked in. He wore pants, boots and an ammunition-filled vest. The fellow was deeply tanned, and Jane was struck by the contrast between his bronzed skin and beautiful white teeth. He smiled at Jane and crossed the room to meet her.

"Did you know that Butch will be home the 20th of August?" The young man whispered the words directly in Jane's ear. She awoke immediately, filled with joy and great confidence that her dream would come true.

Jane was so certain that the message was real that she told everyone she knew about it. She called Butch's young wife, Janice; she told her customers at the salon; she even shared her story with Butch, the next time she wrote to him. When he replied, it was in a brief note, dated August 21.

"I'll be home soon," he wrote. "They picked me up out of a battlefield on August 20th, saying I had orders to go home. Your dream came true, thank God!"

Butch's orders were the result of a clerical error, which was discovered by the time he had reached Da Nang. When he showed Jane's letter to the superstitious officer in charge, however, the man decided to let the orders stand. By September 3, Butch was back on Texas soil.

The family reunion was absolutely joyous. Butch was at last able to hold his tiny baby girl and spend time visiting with each of his loved ones. Jane, grateful to be with her son, listened to every word of his stories. When he brought out photos that he had taken in Vietnam, she examined each of them. One, in particular, took her breath away.

"That's the boy from my dream!" she exclaimed, pointing to a tanned young soldier with a brilliant smile.

Butch looked at the picture and grew pale. That was Wendell, he explained. He was a friend and fellow tank commander. Because of the dangerous land mines that they faced every day, the two would take turns leading the tank column. There had been only one occasion when they didn't adhere to this arrangement.

"It was the day after I got the news that Jamie had arrived," said Butch. "I was scheduled to lead that day. But Wendell insisted on going first. He said 'You've got something to go home for now, with the new baby.'"

It was a generous favor that cost the young soldier his life. Wendell's tank exploded a mine that day, and he was killed along with two of Butch's other army buddies. The young man had sacrificed himself. It may have been the ultimate act of friendship, but it was not his last. Wendell's final kind gesture took place the day his spirit visited Jane, easing her mind with the good news of her son's safe and imminent return.

A Haunting Presence

The people in Sadie Sill's life frequently spoke of the paranormal.

"I felt that someone was near, caring for me all night," many of the patients that Sadie, a nurse, cared for would say.

"We hear mysterious footsteps in the house time after time. We're sure we have a ghost," was the story her parents told.

"I woke George up, screaming," said Sadie's daughter, as she described an apparition that stood at the side of her bed, looking down on her.

Interestingly, Sadie was not only the common denominator in this group, she was the cause of each strange experience. Since childhood, her spirit had traveled out of her sleeping body on countless occasions, often visiting people about whom she cared. "I believe people could see me at times," Sadie wrote, in 1970, "for I could see surprised expressions come over their faces. This would startle me and I would suddenly be back in my own bed."

In the summer of 1968, when Sadie traveled astrally from Lubbock to Corpus Christi to see her daughter, it caused much more than mild surprise. Her daughter became terrified after recognizing her mother's specter and thinking that the older woman must have died. "Mother, you almost scared me to death!" she later scolded Sadie.

The experience may have settled Sadie's roving spirit, for two years later, she admitted that she "rarely [woke] up in strange places" anymore. The strange habit of a life-time had been cured when it became obvious that some people were terribly frightened by Sadie's spiritual visits.

A Terrible Talent

Some people in this world are gifted with psychic, or precognitive, abilities—they are given glimpses of the future. As few who have this "sixth sense" are able to choose what they may prophesy, this ability can be more a curse than a blessing. It is a gift that Emily Welch, who lived her life in Port Arthur, Texas, surely must have wished she had never been given.

The first prediction Emily recalled having came to her in December 1929. She had been up all night, trying to comfort her crying infant daughter. The little girl had been born prematurely and was injured during delivery. Her collarbone had broken and slightly punctured one of her lungs. She was very frail, the doctor had warned Emily. Even a common cold could be fatal to her. These worries played on Emily's mind throughout the night as she cuddled and rocked her baby. By morning the child seemed to feel better, but Emily did not. She spoke to her sister of her concerns, saying, "I have been seeing a little white casket and snow all over the ground."

It was a strange vision, considering the warm climate in which Emily lived. She had seen snow only once in her life. Within less than one week, however, her strange and sad prediction came true. The baby died, and the usually mild temperature plummeted to just a few degrees above zero. As the little girl was laid to rest in her tiny white casket, the cemetery was covered in two feet of snow.

In the spring of 1936, Emily experienced another ominous—and, this time, rather incomplete—psychic message. She was sitting at the piano, concentrating on a difficult piece of music. Her husband was at work, and their eight-year-old son, Billy, was at school. Emily was focusing on the complex arrangement of notes when, suddenly, blood splattered across the page. She jumped to her feet and immediately went to examine her face in a mirror. To her amazement, she found no blood or marks on either her face or hands. When she returned to the piano, she was even more shocked to see that the sheets of music were clean. Emily was sure of what she had seen, however, and felt intuitively that something had happened to her son. She spent the remainder of the day anxiously awaiting bad news.

When Billy arrived safely home from school, Emily was relieved but still checked him over thoroughly. A single spot of dried blood on his shirt collar was the only sign of anything eventful in the boy's day. Emily asked him about it.

"We were playing baseball," Billy said, "and one of the boys made a hit. When he took off for first base he slung his bat and it socked me in the nose. I nearly bled to death, Mom. They took me to the nurse and she put ice on the back of my neck and after a while my nose stopped bleeding."

Emily knew that the moment her son had been hit was the very moment she had seen a shower of crimson drops spray across her music pages.

Nearly 20 years later, in July 1955, Emily received another terrible vision, this time in the form of a dream. She saw her husband lying in the morgue with his head swathed in flesh-colored bandages. The image was so very vivid, Emily was sure that it foretold death. As it turned out, the dream was premonitory, albeit just slightly off the mark. Years afterward, Emily recalled exactly what happened.

"A week later we were called to Louisiana to attend Bill's brother's funeral. Leslie Welch had died on the operating table when undergoing surgery for a brain tumor."

When she viewed Leslie in his casket, prior to the service, Emily was shocked into recalling her vision. "[There was] my brother-in-law," she wrote, "lying with his scalp completely encased in wide pink adhesive tape."

The Black Dog

In British folklore, there is an age-old legend of a spectral dog called "the Black Shuck," a large creature with glowing eyes that haunts cemeteries and deserted back roads. Some say that to meet the Black Shuck is to meet the Devil in canine form. Many believe that the dog is an omen of death and that to even speak of it is bad luck.

In 1962, Wanda Sue Kopec (a pseudonym) met a big black hound that seemed suspiciously supernatural and may have been the "Shuck" of legend. There were two significant discrepancies, however. Wanda Sue met her pooch not on the misty moors, but at the Houston donut shop where she worked. And rather than cursing her, the dog appeared to be her protector.

Wanda Sue worked the night shift. She was alone in the shop long after dark each evening, and she was alone when she walked home along a poorly lit, unpaved street. The young woman knew enough to be cautious: she routinely carried a Coke bottle in one hand and a roll of pennies in the other. She kept her eyes and ears open and hoped that her "weapons" would protect her from harm.

One night, as Wanda Sue was wiping the counters down and preparing to lock the doors of the donut shop, she heard a persistent barking. When she went to the window to investigate, she saw a very large black dog sitting in the parking lot. It was looking directly at Wanda Sue, and it was wagging its tale in such a disarming way that she decided to give it a little snack. She tossed a few donuts outside, then closed and locked the window. Wanda Sue imagined that the dog was a stray that would wander off once it had gobbled up the handout. She was wrong.

Wanda Sue placed the "closed" sign in the front window of the donut shop, locked the door behind her and set off for home, carrying her usual implements of defense. She had walked only a short distance when she began to feel that she was not entirely alone. The tiny hairs on the back of her neck bristled. Her heart quickened. Her feet began to move more quickly along the shadowy stretch of road. She was certain now that she could hear movement in the woods that lined the street. Rustling and a heavy, breathy sound. Panting. The presence closed in, and Wanda Sue spun around to face her pursuer.

It was the dog.

The shaken young woman let her breath out in a whoosh of relief. The black dog was huge and looked fearsome, but Wanda Sue sensed immediately that it meant her no harm. In fact, she felt a little safer walking with her new companion and did not complain when the dog followed her all the way home.

Wanda Sue was renting a small apartment above a commercial wood shop. The landlord had been very specific about not allowing pets in the building. Wanda Sue thought of this and sighed as she turned her key in the lock of the street-level entrance. "I'm afraid you can't come in," she told her canine escort. "It's against the rules." The dog sat down on its haunches and made no further move toward the door. It was as if it understood what had been said.

Wanda Sue opened the door and flicked the switch on the wall. Light from the stairwell spilled out on the stoop.

She turned to take one last look at her new friend and paused. The dog sat there, still and patient. It appeared willing to wait there for her all night. It looked at her with an almost human expression and, for the first time, Wanda Sue noticed the dog's eyes. They were a beautiful shade of sky blue, soulful and intelligent. They were too difficult to resist.

"Okay, okay—it's a bit cold outside," Wanda Sue said as she held the door open for the black dog. "You can stay here tonight, but it's out the door first thing tomorrow morning. Do you understand?" Strangely, she had no doubt that it did. In fact, she could have sworn that the dog nodded before trotting lightly up the stairs to the little apartment they were about to share.

It was to become their routine. Every evening, around midnight, the black hound would meet Wanda Sue at the donut shop. It would walk home with her, along the deserted, dark street and spend the night sleeping on the floor beside her bed. In the morning, Wanda Sue would let the dog back outside before her landlord arrived to work at his wood shop below the apartment. It was a comfortable and mutually beneficial relationship.

On occasion, Wanda Sue would awaken to discover the animal resting its head on her bed, gazing at her with both tenderness and intensity. This could be unnerving, but it was never frightening. She somehow knew the dog would not harm her.

"Of course it wouldn't hurt you. It loves you!" Wanda Sue had invited some friends over for a few beers one night after work. Conversation had eventually come around to Wanda Sue's strange new pet. A girl named Mary, who had drunk a bit too much, was nearly obsessed by the dog's apparent loyalty. "Get over on the couch, again, Andy!" she slurred. "Go try to sit by Wanda Sue!"

The fellow named Andy was uncomfortably perched on top of a wooden crate on the other side of the room but looked completely unwilling to forsake his makeshift seat for a more comfortable spot on the couch. "No thanks," Andy drawled. "I'm fine right here." He had attempted to sit next to Wanda Sue earlier in the evening and had been met with a menacing growl from her shiny, black companion. Wanda Sue had simply shrugged. She was accustomed to the dog's strangely protective behavior. Her friends were not.

"That dog is creepy," Mary pouted, as she wiped at a spill on the front of her blouse. "It's like it knows things. Like tonight!" Mary gestured wildly with her beer bottle, sloshing a little on the floor. "How did it know we were giving you a ride?"

Wanda Sue had no answer for that. She had been worried when the dog hadn't shown up at the donut shop at closing time. She would have stayed a little longer, but her friends had been waiting in the car. It turned out that the dog had been waiting for her, too— sitting patiently at the street entrance of her apartment. It had somehow known that Wanda Sue wouldn't need to be walked home that night.

"That's just plain weird," Mary said, and for emphasis, jabbed her finger in Wanda Sue's direction. Silently, the dog moved in between them. Its lip curled ever so slightly back from its teeth. Mary sank back into her chair. "I'm tellin' you, Wanda Sue," she mumbled. "You want to get rid of that dog."

Did she? Wanda Sue had grown accustomed to the feeling of security that came with having such a large dog around. Perhaps it kept other people at bay, but did that really matter when she worked such long strange hours that she had very little social life anyway? Besides, the dog was quieter than most people, and better behaved. It was almost, well, almost *human*.

Wanda Sue stopped. Was that really how she felt about the dog? Was she letting an animal take the place of human contact in her life? She looked at the black dog, which met her gaze with seductive, hypnotizing eyes. Such vivid blue. Paul Newman eyes, she thought, then silently chastised herself. She really was losing touch with reality if she had started to think of a pet in such terms. Several days later, however, Wanda Sue came to understand why it was that the dog seemed to have so many human qualities.

It was in the early morning hours, after Wanda Sue had returned home from work. The black dog had escorted her, as usual, and was curled up on the worn gray rug beside the sofa. The day had been long and tiring, and Wanda Sue decided that a hot bath might restore her. "I'm going for a soak in the tub," she announced to the dog, and bent over to briefly stroke its smooth head. It looked at her with absolute devotion. As always, the intensity of the animal's expression stirred the slightest feeling of unease within Wanda Sue. As always, she mentally brushed her anxiety away.

The hot water was soothing. Wanda Sue sank deeply into the chipped, old-fashioned tub and felt her muscles relax as her skin turned pink. She was wiggling her toes and watching the ripples they created when she heard the dog coming down the hallway. The familiar click of its toe-nails on the tile was somehow comforting. Wanda Sue closed her eyes for a moment. When she opened them, she was still staring at her toes, but out of the corner of her eye could see the dog's large black shape in the doorway. Suddenly, the pool of darkness seemed to shoot up into the air and fill the entire door frame. Wanda Sue gasped and turned. A wave of water slopped out of the over-filled tub, but she would not notice until much later. Her wide eyes were fixed upon the figure at the bathroom door.

The ebony creature was no longer a dog. It was a man in a black suit. He stared at Wanda Sue with his piercing blue eyes, and in those eyes she recognized the devotion, and possessiveness, that she had been seeing for weeks. She began to scream, and immediately the figure began to change. The shape shifted, the dark lines melted, and the eyes that were staring at Wanda Sue were once again in the form of a dog. She screamed again, and the animal turned and slunk away.

Later, Wanda Sue could not remember how long she sat in the bathtub, with the rising steam and the terrible knowledge that there was some sort of supernatural thing making itself comfortable in her living room. Eventually, she overcame the paralysis of fright and stepped out onto the soaked bath mat. She wrapped herself tightly in the old flannel robe that hung on the back of the door, inhaled deeply for courage, and walked out of the bathroom and down the hall.

The dog-being seemed to be expecting Wanda Sue's reaction, for it had forsaken its usual cozy spot by the couch and was waiting at the door to the stairs. Wanda Sue opened the door and pointed. "Out," she whispered hoarsely. The thing crept out of the apartment and down the stairs. Wanda Sue followed and opened the door to the street. There was a moment of stillness, and she could feel the familiar piercing blue eyes staring at her. She avoided looking back but managed to speak. In a trembling voice, she told the thing, "I don't know what you are, but you have to go. I don't ever want to see you again." It left. Wanda Sue shut and locked the door, then watched through the tiny window as the large, sleek, black shape disappeared into the darkness.

There had been an understanding. Wanda Sue continued to work the night shift at the donut shop but never again encountered the black beast.

Was Wanda Sue Kopec's creature the Black Shuck of legend? While it did not match the profile exactly, there were intriguing similarities. And, to this day, there is no doubt in Wanda Sue's mind that for a few weeks in 1962, she had a companion of the supernatural sort.

The Ghost of "Witch" Canyon

"No part of West Texas is as spectacular or as mysterious as the Big Bend."

Christopher Dow used these words in the opening paragraph of an article he wrote for the January 1985 issue of *FATE* magazine. As he told his story, he clearly illustrated both points. The land, defined by the large bend of the Rio Grande, is spectacular: its rugged, untamed beauty comes clearly to mind with Dow's vivid prose. And this wild area most certainly does have an air of mystery, one that became hauntingly evident to Dow and his friend Charles Roberts during a hiking trip they took in the spring of 1978.

The two had made trips through Big Bend National Park before but this time had chosen to concentrate on new and unfamiliar territory. "This trip," wrote Dow, "we decided to attempt to get on top of Mesa De Anguilla, through which the Rio Grande cuts Santa Elena Canyon. Then we wanted to hike back along the mesa to the river and look down on it from the canyon rim." With their ambitious route in mind, and four days' worth of water and supplies on their backs, Dow and Roberts set out on their adventure.

On the first day of trekking across the challenging terrain, the friends encountered a hostile wild boar and an enormous cloud of wasps. Still, the most fascinating and fearsome sight would not be seen until after sundown when Dow and Roberts had set up camp for the night.

A great, full moon had risen, and it illuminated the magical desert world. When the two men had finished their meal, they settled down on sleeping bags to stretch their tired muscles and survey the beautiful scenery in peace and comfort. They were relaxed and enjoying a good conversation when Christopher Dow became distracted by some movement in the periphery of his vision. He glanced over his left shoulder, expecting to see a tall blade of grass moving in the breeze. He saw nothing.

Dow turned his attention back to his friend, who was still talking. As he did so, he noticed it again—there was something moving, over to his left. He turned to look one more time and, again, saw nothing but the desert, punctuated by a single, scrubby bush. Annoyingly, however, as soon as Dow turned to face Roberts, he could again see movement out of the corner of his eye. Determined to solve the puzzle, he tried a different technique, which he described in *FATE*:

I tried turning my head slowly, watching straight ahead but paying attention to what my peripheral vision brought to me. As my head turned, I was astounded to see a man standing where I had seen the movements! I turned sharply in that direction, but only the scrubby-looking bush was visible. For several minutes I experimented, discovering that if I looked directly at the man, he looked like a bush; but if I watched using my peripheral vision, I could see him quite clearly.

Dow described the man as being short and thickset, with dark features but white hair. He was dressed in the style of a Mexican peasant, with a serape, and a sombrero hanging down his back. More compelling than the man's appearance, however, was his presence. Dow could feel that he "radiated a great power." This sensation of strength was frightening, but Dow somehow felt certain that he and his companion were in no danger.

After about half an hour, Dow felt the presence vanish. As he carefully looked to his left, he could see that the phantom was no longer there watching them. Christopher Dow said nothing to his friend and, soon after, the two travelers grew tired enough to fall asleep under the brilliant and vast desert sky.

The next morning, "without really talking about it," Dow and Roberts decided to abandon the tough trek and hiked back to the little ghost town Terlingua Abaja, where they had left their car. As they put their heavy packs back into the vehicle, Roberts casually asked Dow if he had seen anyone the day before. Dow told him about the mysterious Mexican specter.

After hearing his friend's story, Roberts confessed that he, too, had noticed someone watching their camp. He said that while he had been unable to look at the man directly, he had a fair description of him. Not surprisingly, it matched Dow's exactly. The only difference in their stories was that Roberts had also caught passing glimpses of the man during the afternoon as they had approached the canyon in which they had camped.

The two men traveled back to Houston. Dow later wrote, "It may have been my imagination, but the entire way I felt we were being pursued." They stopped only for gas on the 14-hour drive home.

Dow and Roberts arrived home with only their memories of the trip, for not one photograph taken in the canyon turned out. Other photos on the same roll of film came out perfectly.

Two years later, Christopher Dow, Charles Roberts, and a third friend, Michael Reyes, traveled back to the strange site. They witnessed nothing supernatural on that trip but did make an interesting discovery. "Mike asked a ranger if the place had a name," Dow wrote. "He said it was called Bruja Canyon."

"Bruja," he concluded, "is Spanish for witch."

Chapter 3

Phantoms in
the Family

☠

In many cases when a spirit has been sighted, the apparition is easily recognized as a beloved family member. Though such sightings can be understandably disconcerting, people are rarely frightened by the visits and may take great comfort from them. It's not surprising. After all, it often seems that these souls return specifically to console those whom they have left behind. In other cases, there is unfinished business to attend to, or information or an important message to impart. Perhaps most frequently, these ghosts seem to be watching protectively over their families.

Every spirit that comes back has its own agenda. Sometimes only those who were closest to that person in life will know what reason there may be for a relative's return.

☠

Jim's Last Visit

"That must be Jim!"

It was 1:30 in the morning on a rainy December 19. Nell Sheldon had been awakened by the door bell yet was anything but upset. The cheerful, familiar ringing pattern was only ever used by one person: Nell's son, Jim. The moment she heard it, she knew that Jim had come home to Longview for the holidays.

Happily, Nell threw back the covers and swung her feet off the bed. Before she could move any further, however, she was stopped by her husband, Charles. "Wait, I'll check," he said. "You stay here." Charles put on his slippers, wrapped himself in a robe and went to investigate.

Charles was Jim's stepfather. Much to Nell's regret, the two had never gotten along well, and as she lay in bed that night, she waited for the sound of rising voices. Charles would be irritated at having been awakened, and Jim wouldn't appreciate a hostile greeting after making the long drive from Chicago. There was certain to be an argument. For many long minutes, though, there was nothing but the sound of driving rain. Finally, Charles came back into the bedroom.

"Nobody there, nobody at all," he said, as he slid beneath the covers.

Nell, sure that her husband was lying, was seething. How unjust that Jim should drive all the way home for Christmas, only to be turned away in the midst of a storm! Charles was being cruel beyond belief, Nell thought, as she lay there in the darkness, listening to the pounding rain.

The next morning, the skies had cleared, but the trouble between Nell and Charles had not. Breakfast was eaten silently, as each of them nursed their unspoken resentments. Once Charles left for work, Nell went straight to the front porch, looking for evidence of Jim's visit. She could see no muddy footprints on the freshly painted boards, but that did nothing to change her mind. Only Jim ever rang the door bell in that particular way. He had to have been there.

Nell had cheerlessly begun her chores for the day when she heard another ringing: this time, it was the telephone. Perhaps Jim was calling from wherever he spent the night, Nell hoped. She peeled off her rubber gloves and grabbed the receiver.

"Mrs. Sheldon?"

It wasn't Jim. The voice on the other end of the line was a police officer in Dallas, delivering bad news. Jim had died in an accident early that morning. Nell was needed in Dallas to identify his body.

Nell was grief stricken and shaking. She thought to ask only one question.

"What time did Jim die?"

The officer told her that the accident had happened at 1:30 that morning. It had been exactly the time that the door bell had rung, with Jim's special signal. Nell then knew that it had been Jim at the door after all, coming home one last time.

Ten Cents' Worth of Proof

The elderly woman had suffered a stroke, and her health was rapidly deteriorating. Her days were filled with pain and worry about what would become of her. One night, she dreamed that her late husband had come to visit. He sat in the chair at her bedside, trying to comfort her. "I'll help you," he assured her. "I'll get you through this."

"You can't, darling," the woman responded sadly. "You're dead."

The next morning, the woman recalled every detail of the vivid dream. If only it had been real, she would not feel so alone. Still, a dream is only a dream, she was thinking when she noticed something shiny on the seat of her favorite living room chair. When she picked it up, she saw that it was a dime.

How odd, thought the old woman. She had not been out for two days and so had not opened her purse. The clothing she wore had no pockets from which a dime could have fallen. It was a mystery, but a small one, and was easily forgotten as the day went on.

The next morning, as the woman took her morning coffee into the living room, her attention was caught once more by a glint of silver in the seat of her chair. It was another dime, in the exact same spot. This time, the woman was more concerned than curious. She couldn't understand how this was happening. That evening, before she retired, she counted every bit of change in the apartment and double-checked the seat of the chair.

The next morning, there was another dime.

When she re-counted her coins, she saw that nothing was missing from her change purse or collection jar. It was as though the dime had materialized out of nowhere, but why?

As she pondered this, a distant memory came to her. Long before she and her husband had moved to San Antonio, he had saved a little nest egg for them by collecting dimes. He would break a bill before he would spend a dime. Were the dimes in the chair her husband's way of telling her that he was still taking care of her, that the dream had been real?

Once the riddle had been solved, the dimes stopped appearing. They were no longer needed, as the woman was now greatly comforted by the knowledge that her dear husband awaited her, on the other side.

Grandmother Saved Her

In 1936, young Mary Macey was visiting her parents' home in Texas. One of the things Mary loved best about such visits was that she was able to spend time with her adored horse, Whiskers. The two would take long rides along the Rio Grande, south of La Poloma. It was during one of these rides that Mary ran into a bit of trouble.

Mary and Whiskers accidently came upon a group of men who were unloading crates from a rowboat. "Stop her!" one of them yelled. "If she gets away, she'll tell the cops!" The men were smugglers who had just crossed the Rio Grande from Mexico.

Mary whirled Whiskers around and spurred him into a run. The horse was fast, but the smugglers had a car. Mary heard the engine roar to life behind her, and she knew that if she stayed in the open, they would be able to head her off before she could escape. She tugged on the reins and forced Whiskers to cut a path through the brush. There, she reasoned, the men would be forced to chase her on foot. She was right, but ran into trouble just the same. Only a short distance into the dense brush, Mary and Whiskers ran into a fence. It was a dead end, and the smugglers had them trapped.

Mary listened in terror as the men grew nearer. Then, to her amazement, she heard a soft, familiar voice beside her.

"Don't be afraid."

Mary spun around. Standing there by the fence was her grandmother, Josephine, who had died more than 10 years earlier. The woman smiled calmly at Mary and nodded slightly, as if to assure her that everything would be alright. "Grandma! ... " Mary began. In the wonder of the moment, she had nearly forgotten the danger that she was facing. Fortunately, Grandma Josephine had not.

"Hurry child," the spirit urged. "Get your horse over here in that thick low brush. Make him lie down and you lie beside him. They'll never suspect a horse is hidden in such low brush."

Mary quickly obeyed. She slid out of the saddle and coaxed Whiskers down on the ground. Then she lay silently beside him and prayed that the approaching men would not hear her pounding heart. It seemed that they hid for an eternity while the smugglers searched the area. Finally, the smugglers gave up in frustration and left. When the sound of the retreating voices had finally faded to nothing, Mary got to her feet.

"You were right, Grandma! They're gone!" she cried joyfully. It was then that Mary discovered Grandma Josephine was also gone. Mary was once again safe, but alone.

Nearly 40 years after the incident, Mary Macey wrote about it. She recalled that despite her greatest wishes, she never again encountered the spirit of her loving grandmother. "I prayed she might come and speak to me once more," Mary wrote, "but I never saw her again."

Perhaps it was because Mary never again faced such immediate danger. Almost certainly, however, Josephine continued to watch over her granddaughter—just in case.

Nelly's Father

"I checked my horse, and after one long, straining look around, owned to myself that I was lost."

It was 1880. The traveler on the weary gray steed was winding his way through narrow trails across the plain not more than 30 miles from Dallas, but he was not a native Texan. A newspaper story of the time explained that he was unaccustomed to the territory, unfamiliar with the horse he was riding and found the locals' way of offering directions confusing. "The Texans are a fine people," the man would later write, "but individually and collectively they lack any appreciation of distance. This is due, of course, to them having so much space around them; but to

One traveler, lost on the vast Texas frontier, was guided by a ghost who needed a favor in return.

a stranger ignorant of the extent to which the phrases 'a little piece out' and 'just outside o' town' can be stretched, this contemptuous regard of miles is a little misleading." As darkness descended and looming thunderclouds began to rumble ominously on the horizon, even the traveler's compass became impossible to read. The rain began to fall, and the traveler, who could no longer see farther than his horse's head, decided to give up and simply let the animal follow its own nose. Even the longest night would eventually end, he reasoned. When dawn came, he would once again try to take a logical approach to his dilemma.

The man grew increasingly cold and miserable as the fine rain soaked through his clothing. He cursed himself for having earlier been so arrogantly confident as to "attempt to find anything less than a volcano in active eruption on a bald prairie." The traveler's focus upon his wretchedness was suddenly interrupted, however, when he discovered that he was not alone.

There was a man on the path, about 15 feet in the distance. The traveler felt a surge of relief, quickly followed by curiosity. In the darkness and rain, he could not read his own compass, nor could he see anything else beyond his own horse. How was it, then, he wondered, that he could see this stranger so clearly? How was it that the path directly before him was obscured by the night, yet this fellow was clearly visible as a large man with a heavy red beard, dressed in rough, but well-fitting, clothes? Some trick of the moon and the rain, the traveler supposed, and anyway, did it matter? The important thing was that he had found someone who would lead him to safety, and perhaps even give him shelter for the night. Happily, he called out, "Hello!" The bearded man glanced back with an expression of keen anxiety but did not stop. "Hello, there!" the traveler tried again. Again, there was no response, and the bearded man did not stop. The traveler concluded that his words were being carried away on the wind, and he spurred his weary horse to overtake the stranger. What happened then was puzzling, as the traveler would later recall:

Though the [horse] responded with an alacrity most commendable under the circumstances, I soon found that this strange pedestrian did not intend to let me catch up with him. Not that he hurried himself. He seemed without any exertion to keep a good 15 feet between us.

The effect was eerie. With every stride that the bearded man made, he seemed to skim an even greater distance over the dark path. The traveler was unnerved by the sight but followed along anyway. There was some comfort in having someone to follow, no matter how strange he might be.

We went on in silence for nearly half an hour, when, as suddenly as he had appeared, he was gone. I looked around for him, half-afraid, from his instant and complete disappearance, that I had been dreaming, when I perceived that I was close to a small, low building of some sort.

The place looked cold and deserted, but the traveler was filled with hope nonetheless. It was shelter from the rain and a place to spend the night. His excitement at this prospect was so great that the traveler momentarily forgot about the bearded stranger. He dismounted and tied his horse, then pounded on the door of the little cabin. It was unlatched and swung open easily. The traveler stepped inside, pulled a match from his waterproof case and struck it.

I found myself in a large room close to a fireplace, over which a crude shelf was placed, and on this mantel I saw an oil lamp, to which I applied my match.

On the hearth was heaped a quantity of ashes and over these crouched a child, a little girl of five or six. At the other end of the room which was plainly and scantily furnished, lay a man across a bed, and as I raised the lamp I saw that he was the same I had been following, but there was something in his attitude and face that struck me as peculiar, and I was about to go forward and look at him, when the child who had at first seemed dazed at the light fairly threw herself upon me. "Have you anything for Nelly to eat?" she said, and then: "Oh, Nelly so hungry!"

The traveler produced a paper bag of sweets from his pocket. The rain had turned the wrapper and chocolate into a single pulpy, unappetizing mass, but the child grabbed it hungrily. As she began to eat, the traveler turned his attention back to the man on the bed.

There was no doubt—this was the stranger whom he had been following. The fellow had the same bushy, red beard, the same features, the same clothes. It was the same man, but dead—long dead. One touch proved the stranger's hands to be stiff and cold, and his face had about it a dull gray pallor. The traveler stood staring down at the man, trying to understand how he could have been lying dead in his bed and out walking in the rain at the same time when a small hand touched his.

"Nelly so hungry!" said the child.

"Have you eaten all the candy?" the traveler asked her.

"Yes, yes! But me hungry, for me had no dinner, no brekkus, no supper, and Papa won't get up." Mercifully, the little girl did not seem to suspect what was keeping her father in bed. The traveler gently steered her away from the man's dead body and asked to be shown the kitchen.

The little shack had a small kitchen off to one side, but the shelves were bare of any supplies. Nelly suggested that the traveler look in the shed, outside. This he did, and found a few fresh eggs which he boiled for the child's supper. Once she had eaten, she fell asleep by the fire. The traveler then tended to his tired, wet horse. After that, he performed, as best he could, a simple service for the dead man.

By morning, the rain had ceased. As the light of dawn spilled across the countryside, the traveler was able to see a line of telegraph poles in the distance. He packed his belongings, took the child with him, and was able to follow the line to the nearest town. There, he sought out the proper authorities and notified them of the man's death. As he did so, he learned who the bearded stranger had been.

The dead man's name was Frederick Barnstaple. He was an Englishman, so I found, a recent arrival in these parts. His daughter was restored to her family across the water.

By the time the traveler felt ready to share his astonishing story, Nelly would have been a young woman of 17 years. It was an age she would never had reached had the ghost of her father not seen to his final duty. Nelly's father guided a lost stranger to care for her when he could not. In doing so, the spirit of Frederick Barnstaple may have saved two lives on that dark Texas night.

Cousin Annette

Donna Woodcock was only 16 years old in 1963—the year she experienced one of the strangest events of her life. She had been sleeping soundly in her family's Texarkana home when something woke her. Donna sat up in bed, looked around and saw something she would never forget.

Illuminated in the open doorway of the bedroom was a strange little girl. She wore a blue skirt and white blouse, was barefoot and had a dirty face framed by tangled curls. Donna was frightened by the apparition but pulled the covers over her head, tried to convince herself it was a dream and went back to sleep. Some time later, she awakened again, glanced at the doorway and found the specter of the little girl still there. This time, the child glided across the floor. She passed so closely by the foot of the bed that Donna could have reached out and touched her small white hand. The spirit didn't stop, however, and didn't speak. She simply drifted out of the window on the opposite side of the room.

Donna was still reeling from the experience of seeing an actual ghost in her bedroom when she heard her five-year-old sister, Teresa, scream. The little girl had leaped out of bed and was running through the house as though she was being chased. Eventually, she jumped into bed with Donna.

"What's the matter?" Donna asked, alarmed.

"Nothing," was all the frightened little girl would say. Together, the sisters hid under the safety of the bedcovers and waited for morning.

At the breakfast table, Donna told her mother about the strange events of the previous night. To her surprise, her mother readily believed the story and seemed particularly interested in Teresa's behavior.

"What was it, Teresa," her mother coaxed. "What made you scream?"

Teresa looked up shyly from her plate. Finally, she said, "A little devil touched me right here." She pointed to her forehead. The girls' mother nodded solemnly. Then, she told her daughters something she had never before shared with them.

"Your father and I—we have always had a worry about you, Teresa. We always felt, for some reason, that we might lose you as your aunt and uncle lost little Annette." Donna and Teresa's young cousin, Annette, had drowned at the age of four. It had happened years before, so the sisters had never even met her.

"I believe this is a good sign, though," the girls' mother continued, thoughtfully. "I think it means that we don't need to worry so much about you." The woman never explained exactly how she came to such a conclusion, but the important thing was the incident seemed to ease her mind. As for Donna and Teresa, their strange experience quickly began to fade into memory. They were concerned with other things, for in two weeks, the family was to move to Dallas.

It had been arranged that until a new home was found, the girls and their parents would live with relatives. Coincidentally, it was little Annette's family they were staying with.

On the evening they arrived, while the adults were still

busy exchanging happy greetings, Donna wandered ahead into the living room. A beautifully framed portrait of a child on the center of the mantle caught her attention. "This must be Annette," she whispered to herself, and walked over to have a better look. What she saw drained the color from her face.

It was the little girl she had seen in her bedroom. The ghost who had frightened her, drifted across the room and touched Teresa on the forehead was staring out of the portrait at Donna. It had been Annette who had visited them on that night. As Donna realized this and felt some of the strength drain out of her legs, her parents and aunt and uncle walked into the room.

"Donna! Are you alright?" Donna's mother took one look at her daughter's ashen face and unsteady stance, and hurried over to help Donna to a chair.

"That's Annette," said Donna. It wasn't exactly a question, but Donna's uncle answered, anyway.

"Yes, that's our poor little Annette," he said. After a moment's pause, he added, "You know, we were living in Texarkana when she drowned. In that very house you just moved out of, in fact."

Donna Woodcock had never known Annette and had never seen a photo of her. She certainly hadn't been aware that the little girl had been living in her own family's home at the time she died. But on one strange night, she surely met her spirit. The little ghost had made certain that she shared one astonishing visit with her flesh and blood cousins— before they left her haunt forever.

The Last Piece of the Puzzle

The two women sat side by side in the small, comfortable den, their brows knit in concentration. They were hunched forward over a card table, which was brightly lit from each side by a pair of matching floor lamps. Finally, the younger woman switched off the light beside her, sighed and sank into the pillowy back of the sofa. She rubbed her eyes gently with the middle fingers of both hands.

"There's definitely a piece missing," she said. "I don't know where it could be, Mom."

The older woman nodded and switched off her lamp. She retrieved a cardboard box from the floor by her feet and pointed at the richly detailed picture on its front. "It's part of that rose, right there," she said.

For three weeks, mother and daughter had been working on an elaborate puzzle. With only a few pieces left to put together, it had become disappointingly apparent that one piece was missing. They had searched all over the floor, beneath cushions and even in the clothing they had worn as they worked together each evening. The piece could not be found.

"If your father were here, he would know exactly where to look," said the mother. The daughter agreed. Her parents had built dozens of puzzles together in the den. It had been their favorite pastime. If there was a crevice or corner or shadowy place in that room where a tiny bit of cardboard could hide, Father would know where it was. Unfortunately, the man had been dead for several months and so was not there to help.

The mother and daughter decided to give up for the evening. They would search again the next night, they agreed, when their eyes were fresh.

The two of them moved into the dining room where they shared a light meal. The mother then retired for the evening, and the daughter cleared the dishes and wiped down the table. She looked in on the older woman before leaving.

"Goodnight, Mother," she said. "Sleep well. I'll be back tomorrow night."

She hardly needed to say it, for she had been there every night since her father had passed away. She was a good daughter and simply could not bear the thought of her mother sitting alone in the house, consumed with grief.

The next evening, the daughter walked in the door of her mother's house at the usual time. She did not, however, receive her usual greeting. Instead, she found her mother sitting at the dining room table, wearing an expression so odd that the daughter had to ask her what was the matter.

"Go look at the puzzle," was all the older woman would say.

The daughter walked down the hall to the den and was pleasantly surprised to see that the puzzle had been completed. "You found the piece!" she exclaimed to her mother, who had followed her into the room. "Where was it?"

"It was the strangest thing," said the mother. She went on to explain that when she had been fixing her coffee that morning, she had noticed something shiny in the middle of the dining room table. She picked it up and realized immediately that it was the missing piece of the puzzle.

"But we ate dinner at that table last night," said the daughter. "And I wiped every crumb off when we were finished. There's no way we could have missed seeing it there."

"I know," the mother said mildly. "I know that very well. We didn't see the puzzle piece last night because it wasn't *there* last night."

Suddenly the daughter understood. "Dad heard us, didn't he?" She ran her fingers lightly over the puzzle's glossy surface. "He heard us, and he helped us." The mother simply smiled.

"I think so" was all she said.

It was a small gesture, but it brought comfort and relief. From that point on, the mother's grief seemed to lift somewhat, and the daughter no longer felt compelled to watch over her so closely. After all, her father had not left her mother quite as alone as she had once thought. The last piece of the puzzle proved that he was still nearby and still looking out for them both.

Mary in the Mirror

Joyce Doran of Fort Worth, Texas, will always remember that on one night in 1998, she met one of her fiancé's relatives in a most unusual fashion. It was Friday, December 11, and Joyce had gone to bed early. She slept soundly until 2 AM, then awoke for no apparent reason.

"I rarely do this," Joyce would later write, in a letter to *FATE* magazine, "so I already had an odd feeling. I got a drink of water and decided to read until I fell asleep again."

When Joyce went to the dresser to get a book, some movement in the mirror grabbed her attention. She looked into the glass and was shocked to see that the image staring back was not her own. Joyce would later write of the woman she saw, "I could only see her silhouette, but her hair was nicely styled and she was wearing long sleeves." The vision remained for several minutes—long enough for Joyce to discern that the spectral woman was approximately the same height as Joyce, but a little larger, and that she had her hair pulled up, with a few loose curls framing her face. After Joyce and the spirit in the mirror had regarded each other for quite some time, Joyce decided to wake her fiancé, Dwayne.

"Dwayne, there's someone in the mirror, and it's not me!" she told him. Dwayne mumbled a response but was soon asleep again. Joyce decided that there was no point in staying awake, so she said goodnight to the apparition in the mirror.

On the following Monday, Dwayne received some sad news. His Aunt Mary had died on the previous Friday.

As he talked about it to Joyce, he remembered her odd middle-of-the-night declaration. He asked Joyce if she could describe the woman whom she had seen in the mirror. Joyce proceeded to do so. Dwayne was silent for a moment, then told Joyce that she had just described his aunt.

In her letter to the magazine Joyce Doran revealed what she thought to be the reason for the spirit's late-night visit. She wrote, "I believe [Dwayne's] aunt wanted to see the woman he had decided to marry, since he is the baby of the family."

Aunt Mary must have been satisfied that she saw a happy match, for she never again bothered to peek out of Joyce and Dwayne's bedroom mirror.

Margaret Sends for Help

Josiah Wilbarger felt a fiery explosion of pain at the base of his scalp. With an agonizing scream, he fell from his saddle. Blood began to pour from the wound, soaking the tall prairie grasses in which his crumpled body lay. "I am dying," he thought, with a certain amount of disbelief. When he heard the blood-curdling screams nearby, he knew that his friends were dying too.

He was a man who had good friends, as he was a good friend to others. In particular, he was close to a fellow named Reuben Hornsby, who had followed him from Missouri to Texas in the early 1800s. Wilbarger was not married but enjoyed many of the comforts of family life, through his companionship with Hornsby and his wife and family. He had consumed many fine meals, played with the children and spent many an evening in comfortable conversation by the Hornsby family hearth. Even Hornsby's wife, Sarah, considered the young bachelor a welcome fixture in their lives. Life on the Texas frontier could be hard, but having good friends and neighbors eased the way.

Occasionally, however, even the best of companions couldn't keep one safe.

Wilbarger and four other fellows had been out on a hunting trip. They had ended their expedition and were traveling toward Reuben Hornsby's homestead when their luck ran dry. The group was ambushed by a party of Comanches, who had opened fire on them before they were even aware of what was happening. Two of the men escaped, but Wilbarger's friends Thomas Christian and William Strother were shot off their horses just as he had been. It was their screams he heard as the Comanche warriors slit their throats and claimed their scalps. Temporarily paralyzed as he had been by the rifle ball that lay in the base of his skull, Wilbarger was unable to defend himself or even respond as he heard the braves move in to finish him off. Terrified, he waited for the sensation of steel at his throat. Instead, he felt a hand roughly grasp a handful of hair and jerk his head upward. There was a torturously long minute of exquisite pain as a razor-sharp blade peeled a circle of scalp back from his skull. Merciful blackness followed.

Josiah Wilbarger awoke to discover that he was naked, bloody, in excruciating pain but still alive. Darkness was falling across the quiet plain. The injured frontiersman managed to slowly open his eyes and survey the horrid scene around him. He could see the lifeless corpses of Christian and Strother, and he realized that he had escaped being killed only because the Comanches had thought him already dead. A second, darker, realization was that he may have survived the attack only to die a much slower death exposed to the harsher elements of nature. Wilbarger could barely crawl; he had no food or water; he had no clothing to protect himself from the chill of the night or the day's blistering sun. Reuben Hornsby's place was a good eight miles away, but it might as well have been eight hundred. The situation appeared hopeless. Josiah Wilbarger managed to crawl as far as the nearest tree and prop himself up against its trunk and declare, "It is here I'll die. Here, beneath this tree."

"Nonsense, Josiah Wilbarger."

The voice was feminine and soft and had a playful, scolding tone. "Are such dramatics really necessary?"

Wilbarger could not believe his ears. Slowly, he turned his head in the direction of the voice. There, in the Texas twilight, stood his older sister Margaret. She gazed down upon him with an expression that he remembered so well from his boyhood days when Margaret was like a second mother to the Wilbarger clan. Her hands were sternly placed upon her hips, and she shook her head solemnly. As always, though, there was a twinkle in her eyes.

"You've really done it to yourself now, my brother," she chided.

"This was not entirely my doing," Josiah Wilbarger croaked in defense. The effort of speech brought forth a dry, spastic cough from his parched throat. The pressure lit fresh fire in the wounds on his skull, and Wilbarger cried out in pain. Margaret's face softened into a look of sympathy, and the teasing went out of her voice.

"I haven't much time, dear Josiah, so listen well and heed what I say. I want you to stay here beneath this tree and wait for the help I will send. I promise that you will be rescued before sunset tomorrow."

Wilbarger did listen to what his sister had to say and nodded stiffly to show that he understood. He then forced his aching throat and swollen tongue to form one important question.

"How did you find me, Margaret?"

Wilbarger's sister lived in Missouri. How she had known of his predicament, traveled to Texas so quickly and managed to find him was a mystery. It seemed that it would remain a mystery, for even as Josiah Wilbarger was speaking, Margaret began to walk off into the distance. By some trick of the rising moon, she seemed to drift, effortlessly, across the rough ground. Wilbarger tried to call out and ask her to stay, but the dark curtain within his head was falling again. It would be hours before he regained any level of consciousness.

The next day brought merciless August heat down on Josiah Wilbarger. Several times, he considered crawling away to search for water but stopped himself when he remembered Margaret's instructions. The bit of shade that the tree provided was a blessing, and if only he could hold on until sunset, he would be alright. If only he could hold on.

The shadows were growing long, and Wilbarger began to slip in and out of consciousness. Sometimes he dreamed that the Comanches had come back to kill him. Sometimes, he wished that they would. As the sun began to set, Wilbarger imagined that gentle hands were lifting him onto a buckboard. When he felt a cool splash of water against his cracked, dry lips, he realized that he was not experiencing another trick of the mind. He was being rescued.

"Slowly, Josiah," a familiar voice soothed. "You can have as much water as you want, but only a little at a time. Don't want to cramp up, now." It was Reuben Hornsby, holding the canteen back a little, as Wilbarger clutched at it greedily.

"Reuben, how ... " Wilbarger tried, but was too weak to speak. It would be days before he could tell his strange story or hear the details of his own rescue.

☠

"Josiah, are you feeling well enough to join us by the fire?"

As Sarah Hornsby asked the question, she was already arranging some comfortable cushions in Wilbarger's favorite chair. The man had been in their home for more than a week, recovering from his injuries, and had just managed to take his first evening meal at the kitchen table. He looked tired, but Sarah knew that their friend was anxious to talk about his ordeal. She sent the children off to bed and told her husband that he should pour out a bit of the brandy that was saved for special occasions and medicinal crises. The three friends settled in by the hearth and sipped their drinks. Then the Hornsbys listened attentively as Josiah Wilbarger told his story.

Wilbarger left out no detail—including the vision he

had of his sister, Margaret. He knew that if anyone would believe him, it was Reuben and Sarah Hornsby. When he came to the end of his tale, he said, "That's all I can tell you. But now, I would like to know how it was that you came to rescue me."

The Hornsbys looked at one another. There was a moment of silence, then Reuben began to speak. "You can thank Sarah," he said. "For when we heard about the attack, we had given you up for dead. But then she had, well, I suppose it was a dream. That night, she woke me up saying that you were alive. She had seen you, she knew where you were." Reuben paused thoughtfully, and stared into the fire. Sarah, who had been silent for the entire time they had been sitting together, took up the story.

"It was like a dream, but so real, Josiah. I saw you—pardon me—naked, and bloody, propped up under a big tree. I knew how far away that tree was, and I knew what direction to go. I knew you were alive, and I wouldn't let Reuben rest until he agreed to take some men looking for you." Sarah and Reuben exchanged a knowing look, and Reuben smiled ever so slightly.

"It's true," he admitted. "I had no rest that night."

Wilbarger shook his bandaged head in disbelief. "When did you have this dream?" he asked.

"Not long after I fell asleep," said Sarah Hornsby.

"And I saw Margaret at sunset," Wilbarger mused. "It was like she went for help, as she promised. But how could she have been here, in any form, to help me, when she lives in Missouri and knew nothing of my predicament? It's a mystery, to be sure." As Wilbarger tapped out his pipe and rose unsteadily to go to bed, he shared one final thought with his hosts. "I'll have to write to Margaret about this," he said. "I wonder if she won't have a story of her own, concerning that night."

Before Josiah Wilbarger could put his thoughts on paper, however, he received a letter from Missouri. Sadly, it was notifying him that his dearest Margaret had passed away peacefully in her sleep. The paper shook in Wilbarger's hands as he noted that the date of her death had been the exact day that his hunting party had been attacked. The time of her death, he read, had been sunset.

It was the very hour at which Margaret's spirit had appeared to Josiah Wilbarger, bringing comfort and hope to an injured brother out on the lonely Texas plains.

Family Phoning Home

Spirits frequently communicate with the living through the technological trappings of modern life. Ghosts will often gain attention by meddling with lights, televisions and stereos. Their energy fields sometimes appear as orbs of light on photos or videotapes. It should come as no surprise, then, that the dead occasionally choose to speak with us via our most common means of communication: the telephone. Following are three stories based upon the accounts of Texans who have received *extremely* long-distance calls—in two cases from departed family members, and in one from a close family friend.

☠

"I repeat, will you accept the charges?"

The operator was becoming impatient, but Carolyn was only eight years old and did not know how to handle such a strange situation. She stood in the hallway of the neighbor's house, holding the heavy, black phone receiver uncertainly and scuffing her Sunday-best shoes on the tile. She wished she had not volunteered to answer the telephone.

"Daddy?" she called out to the kitchen, where she could hear her parents carrying on a muted conversation with the other adults. More loudly, then, "Daddy!"

"For heaven's sake, Carolyn! Who is it?" Her mother spoke sharply. Today was a serious day. The children had been told to be respectfully quiet during the visit.

Carolyn stretched the phone cord around the corner, so she could see through the doorway to the kitchen. There, the grown-ups sat around the kitchen table. They all wore conservative church clothes. Carolyn's mother and the neighbor lady wore subdued dresses, nothing like the fresh pastels that all the other women had shown off at that morning's service. It was Easter, but Carolyn knew that there would be no hunt for chocolate eggs in bright baskets of shredded paper. Easter meant something different, now.

"I said, who is it?" All four adults were staring at her now. Everybody knew that it was a great sin to tell even a tiny fib on Easter Sunday, so Carolyn couldn't even hang up and say that it was a wrong number. She would have to tell them.

"The operator says it's a collect call," she said in a tiny voice.

"From whom?"

Carolyn waited a long time before she answered. "From Joyce."

Carolyn's mother made a round "O" of horror with her lips. Her father grew red with rage. The neighbor lady covered her face with her hands. Only the neighbor man spoke.

"Do you think that's funny, Carolyn?" There were tremors in his voice and patches of red and white above the starched collar of his shirt. "Is that some kind of a joke?"

Carolyn was close to tears now. "I wouldn't make that up, Mr. Johnson. I'm just saying what the operator said."

Joyce had been the Johnsons' eldest daughter. On Easter Sunday of the previous year, she had been in a car accident that had taken her life. Now, as the two families were solemnly marking the anniversary of her death, someone who was claiming to be Joyce was making a collect telephone call. It was too horrible.

"What should I do, Mr. Johnson?" Carolyn held the telephone receiver out uncertainly, wanting someone, anyone, to take it away from her. The neighbor man sighed. His chair scraped loudly across the linoleum as he rose. He crossed the kitchen, took the telephone receiver out of Carolyn's hand, and spoke into it with more weariness than anger.

"Who is this?" he asked. There was a moment while he listened. Then, he fainted.

He was a large man, and he came down to the floor with a great crash, knocking over a plant stand and the small telephone table as he went. His wife screamed, and Carolyn's parents jumped up from the kitchen table and hurried over to where the man lay. They crouched on the floor beside him, patting his hands and face. When his eyelids began to flutter, they each took one arm and helped him into the nearest chair. His wife perched on the arm of the chair and stroked his thinning hair. "Are you alright, Bill? Are you alright?" she asked, over and over.

Carolyn retreated to the farthest corner of the living room and watched the action. Her mother went to the kitchen and produced a glass of cool water. Her father righted the plant stand and the table and picked up the dangling telephone receiver. He put it briefly to his ear before replacing it in the cradle.

"Line's dead," he said.

When the neighbor man had drunk the water, and his wife had stopped crying, Carolyn's father dared to ask what everyone wanted to know. "Bill," he said, "who was it?" The neighbor man set his glass down with a trembling hand before he answered.

"It was Joyce," he said, in a small voice. "She said—" he put one hand over his eyes and paused. "She said 'Daddy, I can't get home!'"

There was silence in the room for a long time. Finally, Carolyn's father spoke.

"That was a cruel prank that someone just played on you," he said. "We'll get to the bottom of this, Bill, and whoever's responsible is going to pay."

Bill Johnson shook his head. "It was Joyce," he said, weakly. "I know her voice. Even after all these months, I couldn't mistake her voice."

"It was a prank," Carolyn's father insisted. "I'll prove it to you, and then you'll feel better."

Carolyn's father did try to prove his theory. In the days that followed, he contacted the phone company and had them trace the strange call. There was no record of a collect call to the neighbors' telephone number on that day.

Eventually, both families gave up trying to explain the mystery of how a beloved daughter tried to call home on the anniversary of her death.

☠

Guy Schipper, of Uvalde, Texas, was accustomed to hearing his telephone ring at all hours of the night. He frequently received phone calls from his cousin Pat, a night owl who often forgot that others maintained more regular schedules.

At three o'clock one morning, the persistent ring of the phone invaded Guy's slumber. He groped for the receiver on the bedside table and, without bothering to say "hello," mumbled, "Do you know what time it is?" A familiar voice apologized.

"I'm sorry about that," said Pat, "but there's something I need you to do, tomorrow."

She asked Guy if he would drop by a surgical supply store to pick up a pair of support hose that were on order for her maid. As his cousin made her request, Guy came fully awake. His eyes widened in disbelief. He gripped the telephone receiver tightly and screamed into it.

"Pat!"

There was no answer. The connection was dead, and so was Pat. It had taken Guy a few sleepy moments to remember that his cousin had passed away three days earlier.

The next day, Guy decided to check with the surgical supply store. He found that there had been an order placed by his cousin, and it was ready to be picked up. Guy collected the hose and delivered them to the maid, who was grateful but not surprised.

"I knew Miss Pat wouldn't forget me!" she said.

Apparently she had not. And Pat had also not forgotten her good-hearted cousin Guy, who could be counted on for a favor, even when called upon in the dead of night.

A Dallas family was in mourning following the death of a very dear friend. To make matters worse, immediately after the man's death, they began receiving prank calls in

One communicative spirit attempted to telephone loved ones from his new home: the cemetery.

the middle of the night. Every time the phone was answered at night, the line was silent. Whoever was on the other end would not speak. Repeatedly, the family tried to trace the calls using the tracing feature on their phone, but the feature didn't seem to work, and the calls remained a mystery.

After weeks of disruption, the mother of the family was finally successful in tracing one of the calls. She dialed the number given to her by the phone company, fully prepared to verbally blast whoever had been making the annoying calls.

She was *not* prepared, however, for what she discovered.

The man who answered the telephone was working a night shift—at the cemetery where the family's close friend had recently been buried. He insisted that he knew nothing of the calls, that he worked alone every night and that the phone always sat unused during those hours.

Eventually, the night-time calls stopped. If they had been coming from the family friend, he eventually gave up trying to deliver his message. Unfortunately, as this spirit discovered, the phone service is somewhat unreliable "from the other side."

She Didn't Know

Every night, for three weeks, Tony Fielding received a visit from his sister. That would not have been unusual—the two were very close—but the circumstances were not normal. Tony's sister's visits came in the weeks following her funeral.

It was the mid-1970s, when Tony was 19 and his sister was only 23. As Tony told a reporter for the *Dallas Times Herald*, his sister died quite unexpectedly. The newspaper reported in its October 29, 1991, edition that the young woman was "found lying across her diary, with a whiskey bottle in her back pocket and a trickle of blood coming out of her mouth." No one knew what had happened, and no one was prepared. Tony later came to believe that the least prepared of all was his sister herself.

"After the funeral, just as I was about to fall asleep, my sister would come and stand by my bed," Tony told the *Times Herald.* "It was a hazy, filmy body that you could see through. She looked like she was pleading with me for some reason—so I started asking her what she wanted."

The apparition never answered Tony's question, and eventually he simply told her to leave. When he did, the ghost faded away, leaving "a smoky cloud behind her." Fifteen years later, Tony offered a theory about his sister's spectral visits.

"Many people, like my sister, may not know they're dead. That's why their spirit stays around."

It's not hard to believe that a 23-year-old woman was not expecting to die and was not prepared to pass over to the other side. In this particular case, her spirit remained earthbound for three weeks, until someone cared enough to release her. So many other ghosts have to wait much longer. Sometimes, it takes an eternity.

Chapter 4

Modern
Mysteries

☠

*Some people think that for a ghost story to be truly chilling,
it must take place against the atmosphere of
days gone by. However, contemporary tales—which are
often credible, firsthand accounts of events that occur in
situations and venues familiar to us all—may frighten even
more because they hit so close to home.*

*These stories, from Texas restaurants, hotels, schools,
hospitals and other current settings, offer proof that if you're
looking for a good scare, there's no time like the present.*

☠

The Lady of the Lake

On a moonlit night, White Rock Lake in northeast Dallas is a beautiful place to see—and be seen. Since its construction in 1910, this man-made body of water and the lovely homes surrounding it have been the scene of countless A-list social events. There have been glamorous country club dances, lawn parties and starlit boating excursions. Apparently status isn't everything, however, for a somewhat less prestigious activity may qualify as White Rock Lake's most popular social tradition: parking along one of the deserted roads in search of a little romantic privacy.

The appeal may be that parking near White Rock Lake involves a greater than usual degree of risk. Over the years, many couples who have stopped to "watch the moon shining on the water" have experienced more excitement than they could have imagined or wished for—all courtesy of the local ghost, the specter of a woman rumored to have drowned in the lake in the 1920s.

One young man told of being locked in an embrace with his girlfriend when a fuzzy white light in the distance caught his attention. The light seemed to be approaching their parked car. The couple, worried that it might be a police cruiser, paused to pay attention. Within moments, it became obvious that the glowing object was not another vehicle, but the form of a female, whose gaze was fixed intently upon them.

"Start the car," whispered the girlfriend. The young man, who was busy ensuring that all the doors were locked, didn't need to be told. He fumbled with his keys, dropping them on the dark floor of the vehicle for one heart-stopping moment before managing to jam them into the ignition. The eerily luminous woman was now so close to the couple that she had to bend over slightly to peer in at them through the window. As the engine finally roared to life, she was already reaching, with one shimmering white hand, for the latch on the passenger door. The girlfriend screamed and shrank away from her side of the car. The young man threw the transmission into gear and sped away, spraying gravel behind them. When the couple had put several minutes and miles between themselves and the glowing apparition, they shared a knowing look. Both knew that they had just seen the famous "Lady of White Rock Lake."

Terrifying lovers in their parked cars is one of this spirit's favorite activities, but she has more in her repertoire. She is also famous for hitching rides with unsuspecting motorists, saying that she has been in a boating accident and needs a ride to her Gaston Avenue home. She climbs into the back seat, in her dripping wet white gown, and sits silently during the trip. But when the driver reaches Gaston Avenue and turns to speak to the girl, she is gone, leaving nothing but a puddle of stinking lake water on the seat.

In these cases, the girl appears to be the quintessential vanishing hitchhiker of urban legend. Some stories even follow the prototype so closely as to conclude with the driver approaching the house with the address given to him by the disappearing girl. The door is, of course, answered by a mournful parent who says that the young woman described is their daughter, who drowned in the lake exactly one year, or five years, or 15 years ago that night. These versions of the ghost story are quite easy to dismiss, but others are considerably more credible.

In the April 22, 1964, *Dallas Morning News*, columnist Frank X. Tolbert shared a letter he had received from a reader named Dale Berry. Berry, a sensible-sounding fellow who had purchased a home at the corner of San Fernando Way and White Rock Drive, shared an interesting account of the evening his family moved into the house:

> The first night in our new house the door bell rang. I went to the door. There was no one there. I was very tired, and closed the door. The door bell rang again, "bing-bong." I quickly opened the door and again there was no one there. I waited near the door for a few minutes, and nothing happened. I went back to my moving-in chores, and again the bell rang. This time, my daughter went to the door and stepped out on the porch.

Dale Berry's daughter then screamed, ran back in the house and slammed the door behind her. Berry rushed to her, asking what had happened. She opened the door and showed him. "There were puddles of water as if someone had stood right there dripping, which trailed up the steps and ended in a big puddle right in front of the door."

Berry insisted in his letter that the yard had been dry, and the sprinkler system shut off. When he investigated, he found his property and the street deserted. Could the famed Lady of White Rock Lake have been trying to welcome the Berrys to the neighborhood? It's hard to say.

One of the most famous ghosts in Dallas is the spectral woman who haunts the roads surrounding White Rock Lake.

Dale Berry did save a sample of the water, planning to have it analyzed, but the bottle was somehow lost before he could manage to do so.

In the same column, Frank X. Tolbert wrote that "many sensible and sober witnesses say they've seen this decorative apparition." One woman, a Neiman-Marcus executive who offered the ghost a ride, had such a good look at her that she was able to identify the spirit's soaked gown as being from her own store. In 1985, there were more credible testimonies from a pair of women who were sitting on a dock when they saw the ghostly white-clad figure floating in the water nearby. The corpse rolled slowly over on its back and stared at the women with vacant eyes. Then, with a blood-curdling scream, she vanished.

Those are the types of accounts that make you believe there's something to this story. Of course, they're in the company of hundreds of sightings that have rational explanations. One humorous example: around 1939 or 1940, Dallas Police were mystified by a rash of complaints from motorists traveling on Lawther Drive, the road that circles the lake. All claimed to have been startled by the sudden appearance of a glowing white woman, with outstretched arms, in the middle of the road. The authorities had almost begun to believe in the White Rock Lake ghost when they finally found a logical explanation. At one point along the road, there was an old sign in the shape of a cross. As drivers turned a corner, and their headlights splashed across the sign, it created an eerie image that appeared to be a hovering human form. This is not to suggest that the spectral "Lady of the Lake" does not exist—only that her well-known reputation sometimes precedes her.

The Ghost Doctor of Dallas

In the October 30, 1989, edition of the *Fort Worth Star-Telegram*, reporter Christopher Evans wrote a detailed feature about two paranormal investigators named Terry Smith and Mark Jean. The duo shared many intriguing stories that had come to them in the course of their research, but one in particular stood out. It was a dramatic account that had been told during a taped interview with a medic from a Dallas hospital that had since closed its doors.

The story took place in the summer of 1983. A patient had been rushed to the hospital's emergency room around midnight, with a self-inflicted gunshot wound. The man had taken careful aim, pressing the muzzle of the gun against his cheek so that the bullet would tear away the rear portion of his skull as it exited. By the time emergency crews had arrived, there was little that could be done. Although the man was transported to the hospital and placed on a respirator for a short time, physicians had no choice but to pronounce him dead.

Not long after that, the medic was taking a break in a staff lounge on the second floor. There had always been stories about the second floor of the hospital being haunted by a doctor who had committed suicide, but the medic had never paid them much attention. Just then, however, a nurse walked into the room. She looked shaken and said that she had just seen the ghost doctor.

The staff lounge had large windows overlooking the main hallway. The medic immediately turned to look through the glass and saw a physician whom he did not recognize. In and of itself, that was not unusual, until the medic realized that the physician's "arm was around a patient that he was consoling and talking to, and it was the patient I had just brought it, the one with the gunshot." In other words, the patient who had just been pronounced dead.

The medic was stunned and jumped up to follow the phantoms. They approached a doorway that led to some stairs. Although the two men, side by side, were too wide to walk through the entrance, they effortlessly slipped past. They then turned to climb the stairs. The medic lost sight of the pair and never saw them again.

So, why had the ghost doctor chosen to console this particular new entry to the spirit world? The medic and his co-workers did have a theory. As he told Smith and Jean in his interview, "The man was distraught over family problems, money problems, much the same story as the doctor." They had also both committed suicide in the same fashion. It is touching to think that, in death, one desperate and lonely person managed to finally find someone who truly understood his state of mind: the ghostly doctor, who had once been there himself.

Visions from the Past

When most people hear the word "ghost," they think of a human spirit. Some might also envision the apparitions of animals. Perhaps the definition should be expanded to include things that have no life force, however, for ghostly buildings, vehicles and other inanimate objects are not unheard of. If these soulless things can leave their imprints so strongly upon a place, then perhaps we must rethink what ghosts really are. Perhaps they are not the spirits of people but impressions left by their presence. Whichever way one chooses to define and explain ghosts, though, they remain fascinating. And the ghosts of "things" are sometimes most fascinating of all. In *Montezuma's Serpent and Other True Supernatural Tales of the Southwest* (Paragon House, 1992), authors Brad Steiger and Sherry Hansen Steiger reported a number of spectral buildings and vehicles having been witnessed in Texas.

In one case, a couple by the name of Davidson were vacationing near Corpus Christi when they found themselves attracted to a historic, two-story house overlooking the ocean. Despite the home's well-tended gardens and fresh appearance, it seemed to be vacant. Mr. and Mrs. Davidson, who wanted to spend their summer in the area, hoped that the place might be for rent. They didn't have time to investigate at that particular time but took careful note of the house's location and vowed to return later.

Only a few hours had passed before the Davidsons were back on the same street, looking for the tidy, old-fashioned house. On their second visit, however, the place was nowhere to be found. The Steigers quoted Mr. Davidson as saying, "We drove all over the area, but we saw nothing even resembling that magnificent old house. When we spoke to the nearest neighbors, we could find no one who had even a memory of such a house ever having been in the neighborhood."

Another "phantom building" spoken of in the book was different in that it came complete with ghostly residents. It was a restaurant, a few miles east of Amarillo. Sam and Clara Carter stopped there in the pre-dawn hours of a May day in 1987.

Though the Carters were familiar with the area, neither had ever noticed this particular "quaint, rustic-style restaurant" before. They decided to give it a try and were delighted with what they discovered. The food was superb, and the service incredibly friendly. The Carters chatted with both the waitress and cook and promised that they would definitely make a return visit. They were not able to make good on that promise, however, because despite numerous trips up and down that same highway, the Carters were never again able to find that deserted little cafe.

In the Carters' experience, there were at least two human ghosts (the waitress and the cook) associated with the phantom restaurant. In one of the Steigers' other stories, a spectral vehicle came complete with the apparition of a driver.

It was 1986. Lyle Mortensen and his family were driving near Galveston when they pulled up behind an old Model-T Ford. The antique car was traveling so slowly that traffic began to back up behind Mortensen's vehicle. After waiting patiently for a while, Mortensen realized that the driver had no plans to pull over and courteously let the other vehicles pass. In frustration, he gave a blast of his horn.

The driver of the Model-T was visibly startled and looked over his shoulder to see what was behind him. Lyle Mortensen saw the man's face twist in an expression of terror. Then the old car "seemed to drift sideways off the road" and ended up in the ditch. Mortensen was mortified, certain that his impatience had caused the other driver's accident. "I've got to go back and see if he's alright," he told his wife.

It was soon obvious that nothing could be done. As Lyle Mortensen pulled over to the shoulder of the road alongside the Model-T, the car began to fade from sight. The Mortensens later estimated that it took about 30 seconds for the very real-looking image to vanish completely.

Dating back to 1960 there's a story of a ghost train that did not fade away but simply traveled out of sight. The witness, Thomas Phillips of Pasadena, realized that the train was not of this dimension.

The first thing Phillips noticed as he sat in his car waiting for the train to pass was that there were no crossing lights, signs or signals marking the spot where the old-style locomotive crossed the highway. He then observed that the freight cars seemed to be glowing slightly, lit by something other than his own headlights. What really shocked Phillips, however, was what he saw after the last boxcar had passed. With the train gone, he could clearly see that there were no tracks and no sign that a railroad bed had ever been set across the highway at that point.

Just a few more ghostly "things" to consider in the haunted state of Texas.

School Spirits

The original Metz Elementary School in East Austin was built during World War I. For more than seven decades, classes were taught there, until the building had fallen into such disrepair that there were concerns about the children's safety. Finally, in 1990, the funds were available to build a new school on the old site. Parents, students and members of the faculty were all thrilled with the plan. It was not until the fall of that year, as demolition of the old Metz began, that any opposition became apparent. When construction crews and heavy machinery began wrecking the 74-year-old building, it seemed that the spirits of former students were standing in the way.

Joe Torres of Torres Trucking and Excavation noticed something odd the first time he walked through the old school. As he and his son Gabriel surveyed the deserted halls and classrooms, planning the demolition project, they heard several mysterious sounds. "We heard scratching on a chalkboard," Torres told the *Austin American-Statesman.* "We thought we heard kids playing in the classroom, but no one was around." The strange echoes were perplexing but were not enough to distract Torres. He told himself that there was some logical explanation and went about his business.

Within a short time, however, the peculiar events at Metz had begun to affect Torres's business. Workers began to complain that their ladders were moving, as though they were being shaken by unseen hands. On one day alone, five pieces of heavy machinery failed, in rapid

In 1990, construction of the new Metz Elementary School was put behind schedule when the spirits of former students seemed intent upon bringing demolition of this old building to a halt.

succession. The truck that was dispatched to pick up replacement parts for the equipment then broke down as well. Later on, mechanics were able to find little wrong with the various machines. That was small consolation to Torres, who had already lost $3000 in lost working time.

The equipment problems and unusual accidents became so commonplace at the Metz job site that it wasn't long before some workers were thoroughly spooked. When some of Joe Torres's laborers refused to go back into the crumbling old building, he took another walk through the halls himself. Again, he heard the eerie, hollow sounds of children laughing and playing. There were sounds of wooden chair legs scraping across the bare floor and of chalk scratching against a blackboard. Torres searched the building completely, hoping to find some explanation. He found none but still resisted believing that the small spirits of former students were standing in the way of his project. "It might be a coincidence," he said, afterward. "It's kind of hard for me to swallow."

The theory was much more easily accepted by Elaine Ireland of the Central Texas Parapsychology Association. Ireland told the *Austin American-Statesman* that the general area in which Metz Elementary was located was known as a site of intense paranormal activity. Furthermore, she explained, "The school was full of love and laughter and a part of that energy is still there. School is a haven for a lot of children. It's like tearing down their home."

Eventually, whether Joe Torres believed in the ghosts or not, he had to admit that he had a problem. He hoped that a lay evangelist named Elias Limon from the Casa Guadalupe Catholic Center would be able to provide him with the solution. Limon spent some time at the construction site, in September 1990, armed with holy water and blessings. He prayed that "whatever [had] not found rest would find rest." Everyone hoped that would be the end of the unnatural activity at Metz Elementary. It was not.

According to *Haunted Places: The National Directory* (Penguin Books, 1996), the problems actually became more serious. Author Dennis William Hauck wrote that a short time after the religious ceremony was performed, a man was killed on-site "when a wall 'exploded' on him." Ultimately, the project was plagued with so many setbacks and so much bad luck, it finished nearly six months behind schedule.

And, as for Joe Torres's reluctance to believe in the supernatural? In September 1990, he told reporter Julie Bonnin of the *Austin American-Statesman*, "I'm not a superstitious person, I'm too old to believe it, but you walk through and think, if these walls could talk." Two years later, when all was said and done, something happened that may finally have converted the level-headed foreman into a believer. According to author Dennis William Hauck, Torres transplanted a tree from the grounds of Metz Elementary to the front yard of his daughter's home. Hauck stated, "Now, people claim to hear the voices of children coming from that tree."

The Reaper

Though hospitals are places of healing, they are also frequently places of death. No one can attest to that more than the nurses who tend to every need of the sick and dying. Perhaps this close contact that nurses share with their patients is the reason so many of them have witnessed paranormal incidents taking place at a deathbed. One chilling story was told to *Strange Magazine* in 1997 by a private-duty nurse who worked in a Houston hospital.

The nurse had just arrived at the hospital and was hurrying down the hall toward her patient's room. Anxious to relieve the other person on duty, the woman was almost too preoccupied to notice a strange, dark figure standing in one of the rooms she passed. Several feet past the doorway, however, the nurse stopped short.

If she had really seen what she thought she had seen ....
Suddenly unconcerned about the time, the woman
turned and retraced her steps.

The nurse stopped in the hall outside the room and
peered through the doorway. An old, gray-haired woman
lay in the bed, supported by a nest of pillows. Standing
patiently beside her was a still, tall, black-robed being
that made the nurse catch her breath in utter shock.
When it lifted its hooded head and looked at her, she felt
her blood turn to ice. She had just made eye contact with
the Grim Reaper.

The creature's face was a skull, and its eyes were glowing red coals. It was the very image of patience, with its
skeletal hands folded together and the quiet composure
of one who is willing to wait as long as necessary. As the
terrified nurse looked into that ghastly visage, she was
overwhelmed by the stench of rot. *That's the smell of death,*
she thought, then broke away from the Reaper's horrible
gaze, turned and quickly walked away.

When the nurse arrived in her own patient's room, she
was pale and trembling with cold. The male nurse whom
she was scheduled to relieve took one look at his shaken
colleague and immediately wrapped her in warm blankets.
He then gave her a hot drink and waited patiently for an
explanation. It was nearly two hours before the frightened
nurse was able to tell her co-worker what she had seen.
Once she did, he simply nodded. "That lady has been
fighting death for over seven days," he said.

Soon after, the old woman passed away. The Reaper's
wait was over.

The Night-shift Visitor

Another story of a haunted hospital took place in a small facility in rural Texas. A woman named Noreen Pfister, who once worked the night shift in the general admitting office, would later write of a strange experience that she had over the course of several January nights.

It started on one particularly cold night, when the dull moan of the winter wind could be heard outside the hospital's windows and doors. Pfister was doing some paperwork at her desk around 2 AM when she heard the front door squeak loudly on its hinges. The sound of the wind intensified briefly, and a blast of icy air reached the office. Someone slowly made his way down the hallway toward the office, and the sound of boot heels on the marble could be heard. Then there was a pause and the scraping sound of a foot being shuffled sideways as the visitor turned to face the admitting office window.

It was only then, when she knew that the late-night visitor was waiting to see her, that Pfister finally rose from her paperwork. But when she walked over to the window, she found no one there. Pfister leaned out of the window and scanned the hall, up and down. It was deserted. Cursing her imagination, she returned to her desk.

The incident might easily have been forgotten if it hadn't happened again. But the very next night, Pfister was mystified by the same sounds of the opening door and slow, deliberate footsteps. Again, she heard the rub of leather on the floor as the visitor turned on his heel to face the window. And, again, no one was there to be seen.

The phenomenon occurred on a regular basis. Pfister was understandably curious and anxious to solve the mystery. She grilled her co-workers, trying to determine if someone was playing a trick on her. She got in the habit of rushing over to where she could see the front door whenever she heard it open. Still, she found no rational explanation for the strange, disembodied footsteps.

One night, Pfister happened to be away from her desk when the ghostly visitor arrived. From where she was, she had a full view of the front door and hallway leading up to the office window. What Pfister saw—or rather, didn't see—astounded her.

As usual, her attention was caught by the loud squeaking of the door's hinges. She looked up to the sound of the door slowly closing but could see that it was actually securely shut. Then came the footsteps. Although she could clearly see that no one was there, Pfister heard the slow walk down the hallway and the sound of a boot as its wearer turned to face the window. It was then that Noreen Pfister decided to speak.

She greeted the spirit warmly and invited it to sit down with her. "Stay as long as you like," she said. "I'm lonely, too."

It was the last time that the ghost in the cowboy boots dropped by, but Pfister felt that a warm, peaceful presence remained with her. "I have never felt alone or lonely since," she wrote. "I have a friend."

And so does the spirit whom she welcomed into her life.

The Jury Believed

It sounded a whole lot like the movie *Poltergeist*.

In 1983, Sam and Judy Haney decided to have a swimming pool installed in the back yard of their Crosby home. What they were looking for was a pleasant place to cool off on hot summer afternoons. What they found were human remains.

In the course of excavating the yard, the Haneys discovered that their home had been constructed atop an abandoned, 1920s-era cemetery. The find was not only undeniably gruesome, it also led to numerous strange events that, collectively, could only be described as "a haunting." Not knowing where to turn for help, the Haneys eventually took an unconventional approach to solving their paranormal problem. They decided to put their faith in the legal system and sue the developer of their property.

In the summer of 1987, jurors in a Houston courtroom spent a week listening to testimony from the Haneys and their neighbors. They heard tales of ghostly apparitions that wandered the properties near where the remains had been found. They learned that the Haneys' television set randomly turned on and off in the middle of the night. They were told that Judy Haney's shoes once disappeared from her closet and mysteriously reappeared, side by side, next to one grave. Finally, they were asked to find the Haneys deserving of two million dollars in compensation.

In the end, the jury decided in favor of Sam and Judy Haney but suggested that their mental anguish had a price tag of only $142,000. It would be interesting to know how they arrived at that figure in a case so lacking in precedent.

Possessed Possessions

So, you think your house is haunted? Don't be so sure. Some people who have lived with a ghost eventually discover that the entity was not attached to the house but to something within it. People who love to furnish their homes with unique and charming bargains from antique stores and second-hand shops may think twice about their buying habits after reading these two tales of "possessed possessions" in Texas.

☠

In 1974, a woman named Glenn E. Newton wrote to *FATE* magazine about a strange event that had taken place in her family's farm home near Cleveland, Texas.

According to Newton, it all started in 1969, after her children had grown and moved away. She had decided to turn her sons' bedroom into a guest room and went shopping for a suitable double bed. Newton found one at a used furniture store in Cleveland. She purchased the bed, took it home and set it up in the newly designated guest room. Not long afterward, she experienced the first of many strange happenings.

Newton explained that she had been home alone one evening, sitting in a chair opposite the door that opened into the guest room. A noise caught her attention, and she looked up in time to see the door to the room open. Newton was ready to dismiss that as the work of a draft until she heard the sound of footsteps coming out of the guest room toward the place where she was sitting. Newton jumped up and ran out to the screened front porch. There, she stood where she had a clear view of the living room in which she had been sitting.

"The steps crossed the room and stopped beside [my] chair," Newton wrote. "The room was well lighted, but I could see no one there. After a pause, the footsteps went back to the guest room door, and the door closed. For fear of being ridiculed, I mentioned this strange occurrence to no one."

A few months later, the Newtons' daughter Edith brought her new husband out to spend a weekend at her parents' farm. The young couple slept in the guest room. Following their first night there, Edith took her mother aside and mentioned that her husband had expressed concern about having his parents-in-law walking around in the guest room in the middle of the night.

"I assured her neither of us had been in there," Newton wrote. Edith passed her mother's assurances on to her husband.

On the second night of the newlyweds' visit, the footsteps returned. This time, Edith's husband leaped out of bed and followed the sound, which traveled through the house and ended at the dining room table. "After this incident," recalled Newton, "the walking was heard by everyone who spent the night in our home." The door to the guest room also continued to open and close frequently on its own.

For three years, the Newtons lived with the eerie footsteps and were at a loss to explain why they had begun. They had given up searching for an explanation or a solution when Glenn Newton decided to make some further changes in the room. She found a bed that she preferred to the one she'd purchased three years earlier in the second-hand store. The new bed was set up in the guest room, and the old one was put out in the yard until the Newtons could decide where they wanted to store it. That problem was immediately solved when Edith's brother-in-law, Clyde, dropped by and offered to buy it. He took the bed home that very day and set it up in his own guest room.

A month or so later, Edith dropped by to visit her mother. Casually, she asked if either of her parents had heard the ghost walking around recently. Glenn Newton had to stop and think for a moment. The phantom footsteps had become so much a part of their lives that she and her husband barely bothered to take note of them anymore. After careful consideration, though, Newton realized with some surprise that it had actually been several weeks since the walking spirit had been around. Edith felt that she knew why.

"You sold the ghost to Clyde," she said.

Edith went on to explain that her brother-in-law and his wife had begun to hear the same strange footsteps that had, for three years, wandered through the Newtons' home. In addition, the door to the room where Clyde had set up the bed was now opening and closing, seemingly of its own volition.

As time went on, it became apparent that the ghost really was connected with the old bed. The Newtons never heard the footsteps again in their home, but Edith's brother- and sister-in-law continued to be tormented by the mysterious sounds. In all likelihood, the unlucky people were eventually informed about the source of their newfound specter, but they were still in the dark at the time Glenn Newton wrote her letter. She was letting Edith choose the right time to disclose the information, noting that her daughter was worried that "they always would feel I knew the bed was haunted when I sold it to them."

That's understandable. Dealing diplomatically with in-laws can be a delicate business—perhaps even more so where matters of the supernatural are concerned.

☠

In the summer of 1973, a large shipment of antiques made its way from Britain to America. One of countless items on board was a small, darkly finished, wooden table, with three gently curving legs and a delicately carved floral design. By the time the table arrived at a Pier 1 store in Dallas, the piece was slightly damaged. Store manager Weldon Maxey wasn't concerned. He repaired the table with a little glue and sold it to a Southern Methodist University student for $29. Maxey was certain that the student would enjoy his new purchase. Within weeks, he would discover that he had been wrong.

The young man made a mysterious phone call to the store one day. He said that he wished to return the flower-carved table. When asked why, the student quickly hung up. Some time after that incident, he called back and again asked that the store reconsider its no-returns policy in his special case. This time, the student stayed on the line long enough to offer an explanation: he claimed that the table was haunted.

"He said it turned the lights and water on and off in his house, and he would wake up in the morning and all religious articles, save those that were blessed, would be turned over," Weldon Maxey explained in an article in the November 4, 1973, *Dallas Morning News*. Maxey made an exception for the student and refunded his money for the table. Then, curious about the claims that the customer had made, he took the antique piece home. Soon, strange things were beginning to happen in Maxey's house as well.

"One night my wife was reading, about 1 AM, by herself," Maxey told Michael Fresques of the *Morning News*. "She felt definite pressure on her arm, three or four times."

That was more than enough to convince the Maxeys that they did not want the little table in their home. Back to the store it went, along with its resident spirit and its growing reputation.

The story of the haunted table was beginning to get around and, before long, people were coming to the store expressly to see the piece and ask questions about it. Many would run their hands lightly over its carved surface, trying to feel "hot spots" of spiritual activity within it. According to the *News*, "One elderly customer came into the store ... put a plastic box on the table, then quickly picked it up, slammed a lid on it, announced 'Now, I've got your ghost,' and walked out of the store." Perhaps even more eccentric was the man who offered to pay the store $500 if they allowed him to borrow the table for just one night.

There were those who had serious professional interest in the table as well. Various Dallas mediums and spiritualists conducted séances or readings about it. Several suggested that the soul of a small child was contained within. One psychic and automatic writer, Sadie McCollum, agreed with those findings—but said that there was another, darker spirit that was predominant.

McCollum knew because a disturbing vision of the being, a 16th-century Prussian man, had appeared to her in her home. She described the entity as "a hideous thing," saying he had "huge holes for his eyes and long nails that turned under at the ends, [and] long, stringy hair." The creature begged McCollum to help him escape from his strange, small prison. McCollum arranged to visit the store and perform an exorcism.

When the day came, Sadie McCollum sat before the table with famed New York parapsychologist and author Hans Holzer. They had been discussing the case and agreed that the ghost had been held captive ever since the Prussian man's death, some 400 years earlier. It was time, they felt, to free the tortured soul, and they began the ceremony with an automatic writing session. McCollum sat entranced with a sheet of white paper before her and a pen placed loosely in her fingers. The sensitive's hand began to move—slowly, at first, then gaining speed—and words were scrawled across the page. The transcript was printed in the *Dallas Morning News:*

I will leave now forever. This is William Vladistok of Prussia. I thank you. You are a brave soul. My nature is profoundly evil and I have for many years exercised the practice of evil. Take the word of God as the ultimate for all and henceforth make no idle sayings for which I am responsible.

Remember you have freed me. You can and will progress with your most fond wishes. I shall be gone from this table within 3½ hours from this moment. Kindest regards, dear lady. Adieu.

Sadie McCollum stopped writing and put both hands upon the table. "It's moving inside," she told reporter Michael Fresques. "There's a sort of heartbeat here." McCollum then proceeded to speak directly to Vladistok, directing him to "take leave of the table. Burst forth to God and peace." Then, with one loud final command to the spirit—"COME OUT NOW!"—it was over.

When Sadie McCollum had finished her work, she assured Weldon Maxey that the spirits of both Vladistok and the small child had been successfully exorcised. Maxey was pleased. He polished the table, put it back in the show-room and offered it for sale once more. This time, however, the newly cleansed table carried a price tag of $1500. It was probably fair. After all, that's the kind of specialized refurbishing that a person just can't do at home.

Spirits With Dinner

The Catfish Plantation Restaurant in Waxahachie, south of Dallas, doesn't serve liquor with its famed Cajun cuisine. You are welcome to bring your own, though—or you could stick to soft drinks and keep a sharp eye out for the type of spirits you won't find on any bar menu, for this is undoubtedly the most haunted restaurant in Texas, if not all of the United States.

When Tom and Melissa Baker opened their popular business in the converted Victorian house, they had no idea that there was anything out of the ordinary. That was 1984. In the years since, their charming eatery has been found extraordinary enough to be featured in numerous books, newspapers and magazines, and on both local and national television programs. And while the food is good, the publicity is undeniably owed to the three ghosts who haunt the restaurant.

The Bakers began to suspect that they had spectral tenants about two months after moving in. It began when Melissa opened the restaurant one morning and was greeted by the smell of just-brewed coffee. Indeed, there was a full, fresh pot waiting to be consumed—which might have been nice had it not been so mysterious. After all, Melissa was the first person to arrive at the restaurant and the only one who had a key. Still, strange as that incident was, she wrote it off as a prank. The whole thing might have been forgotten if nothing similar had subsequently happened. A few weeks later, Melissa unlocked the doors to discover a large steel tea urn that was normally kept on a shelf sitting in the middle of the kitchen floor. Inside it, dozens of coffee cups had been carefully stacked. "Again, I thought this was a trick," Melissa told Arthur Myers, in his book *A Ghosthunter's Guide* (Contemporary Books, 1993). But when employees began to report scores of similarly unusual events, she had to think again.

Servers were saying that they had actually seen coffee cups floating across the room and wine glasses leaping off the shelves by themselves. In the washrooms, the toilet seats lifted up as though they were spring loaded, the toilets flushed automatically and water gushed out of the faucets when the taps had not been touched. Lights flickered. The burglar alarm would be mysteriously triggered. The radio changed stations by itself. Place mats, napkins and silverware that were carefully set out at night would be in a state of disarray come morning, and icy cold pockets of air seemed to wander through the dining rooms.

The kitchen staff had complaints of their own. Pots and pans frequently came flying off the shelves, no matter how carefully they had been put away. Someone was hit in the head with a piece of cheese when no one else was in the room. A container of chives traveled across the kitchen, sprinkling its contents on the floor as it went. Then there was a basket full of french fries that lifted itself out of the deep-fryer and hovered magically in the air.

The bizarre evidence was mounting. Many people who worked at the Catfish Plantation were beginning to suspect that there were phantoms present. But, despite the rash of supernatural events, Melissa Baker resisted believing that there was anything paranormal going on in the restaurant. "I'm not a metaphysical follower," she told

Michael Precker of the *Dallas Morning News.* "I didn't believe in ghosts. I really started to think I had hired a bunch of kooks to work here. But things continued to happen."

Eventually, Melissa was concerned enough to consult with a psychic and a team of paranormal investigators. She also commissioned some historical research on the house. Ultimately, Melissa was amazed to note that the information that had come by way of numerous séances agreed with details from more traditional archives. All sources indicated that the Catfish Plantation was haunted by three distinct spirits, all of whom had died in the house.

The first was a young woman named Elizabeth Anderson, whose father had built the house in 1895. She died on her wedding day in the 1920s when a former lover strangled her to death. It was poor Elizabeth's apparition that customers sometimes saw in the bay window overlooking Water Street. Her presence was often announced by the scent of roses, and she projected a feeling of sweetness and gentleness. She was soon best known as the ghost most likely to touch people. Recipients of her caress usually experienced it as a cool, tingling sensation. Melissa Baker once recalled a particularly dramatic experience. "I was counting the money and doing my paperwork," she told author Arthur Myers, "and I got this cold sensation on my right hand. It was just on that hand. I feel Elizabeth was holding my hand while I was working. This went on for about 15 minutes."

The Bakers discovered that their second specter was a farmer named Will, who had lived and died in the house during the Great Depression. By far the least active spirit,

Will was just quietly present in the house. His presence likely produced cold spots but, aside from that, the old fellow didn't seem to be responsible for any noticeable paranormal activity. If Will had been the only entity in the house, the Bakers would probably not have been aware that they had a ghost. The same could hardly have been said of their third spirit, Caroline.

Caroline was the last resident to die in the house. She was an elderly woman who died after having a stroke in 1970, and she stayed on to become, definitely, the most disruptive ghost. Melissa Baker described her as their "thrower and slammer," known for her hot temper and her inclination to take her frustrations out on the glassware. Psychics suggested that Caroline would get upset with the number of strangers who traipsed through what she still regarded as "her" house. They also said that she spent a good deal of her life in the kitchen preparing family meals. After her death, when her family would fail to appear for dinner, she was apt to have a tantrum.

While she never actually "appeared" as often as did Elizabeth, Caroline was seen by customers on at least one occasion. Zinita Fowler, in *Ghost Stories of Old Texas III* (Eakin Press, 1995), wrote of a time when a carful of people arrived in the restaurant's rear parking lot. As they got out of the vehicle, they noticed an old woman dressed in black beckoning to them from the back door. To be polite, the people waved at her but went around to the front entrance. Once seated, they asked their server who the woman in black was. They were told that no one of the elderly lady's description worked at the restaurant, although someone who looked just like her did haunt the place.

It was not easy for the Bakers to decide to share such information with customers. Even once Melissa had been convinced that the ghosts were real, Tom, who spent less time at the restaurant, remained uncertain. Then, even after Tom started to believe, the couple was unsure how the information, if it became public, would affect business. Eventually, the matter took care of itself. So many mysterious things were happening to diners at the Catfish Plantation that denying the ghostly rumors would have been impossible. So, instead, the Bakers chose to embrace the idea of having a haunted restaurant. They handed out pamphlets about their resident spirits and mentioned the haunting in their advertising. They left a notebook out in which people could jot down strange things that happened to them in the restaurant, and they put up a sign saying, "If you have a ghostly experience, please tell us!"

Customers responded enthusiastically. They wrote about being touched by icy hands, having items pulled out of their pockets and watching in amazement as dollar bills, placed on the table for a tip, rose and hovered in the air. One person claimed that a spoon leaped off the table and struck the wall. Another noted, "While sitting and reading to my son Drew about the ghosts, my purse turned upside down and dumped everything, from [the] side pocket too, on the floor."

Not all of the incredible events have been included in the notebooks, however. One couple was so spooked that they left without finishing their meals, let alone making a note of their experience. They had been in the Catfish Plantation with their baby, whom Melissa had stopped to admire. She asked the child's name and was told it was

"Alicia." A few minutes later, the people were clearly frightened and preparing to leave. When asked why, they pointed to a window. There, in ghostly script on a patch of condensation, was the name "Alicia." The couple told Melissa that they thought the restaurant was lovely, and the food had been enjoyable, but that they would never be back again.

Fortunately, most people feel otherwise. Any initial concerns that the Bakers may have had about negative publicity have proven to be unfounded. The ghosts have provided many promotional opportunities, and customers by and large seem to enjoy the idea of dining in a haunted place. In October 1994, the *Dallas Morning News* quoted Melissa Baker as saying, "It's been great. I guess it's entertaining. I hope people come for good food, but a lot of them come expecting something to happen."

Many diners who took such expectations to the restaurant left satisfied. Patrons have had countless paranormal experiences, although the phenomena have slowed down over the years. Melissa Baker has theorized that it is because she and her husband and staff reached out to the spirits instead of allowing themselves to be frightened off. "They just seem to want attention," she told the *Morning News*, "or just to let us know they're here."

The ghosts must be pleased, for certainly by now, there are few people who *don't* know about the otherworldly antics at Waxahachie's famous, haunted Catfish Plantation.

Chapter 5

Tall Texas
Tales

☠

*Some Texas ghost stories have been around for so long,
and have been told so many times, they must fall into the
category of "legends and folklore." This is not to say they are
fiction—every story begins with a real event of some sort,
and even those that have been most richly embellished likely
have, at their core, a grain of truth. It is simply that they are
so widely known, oft repeated and accepted that unites these
tales in a class of their own.*

*Read on, and you may recognize a yarn once told to you by
a grandparent or older sibling by the eerie flicker of a candle's
flame. The details may change, but the essence of the story
always remains the same, in these tall Texas tales ...*

☠

La Llorona: The Weeping Woman

The sky, bruised with thunderclouds, is split every so often by a bolt of electricity. Wind howls and moans as it grapples for loose shutters and shingles. When the rain finally begins to pour down, it is torrential, drenching the land and battering the rooftops.

The storm is frightening, but the children who huddle indoors are more frightened of the legendary, shrouded figure who is said to walk by the water's edge whenever the weather turns violent. Her cry is lonely and beckoning; her search for young children is eternal; her name—is La Llorona.

☠

La Llorona, a mournful and much-feared ghost, is a fixture of Mexican and Mexican-American folklore. She is said to be the specter of a woman who long ago drowned her three young children in order to please a lover who did not want the burden of a family. After committing the deed, she was overcome with guilt and threw herself into the same churning river where she had murdered her babies. Ever since, her weeping spirit has been doomed to haunt the banks and shores of lonely waterways, endlessly seeking her lost little ones. It is said that no children are safe when she is near. La Llorona will capture any youngsters who come her way, luring them into her watery grave.

In most versions of this eerie story, La Llorona is a seductive figure in black, with long dark hair, and claws for fingernails. The tale does tend to vary, however, from region to region. In El Paso, the ghost wears a flowing white gown and is faceless. In other parts of the state, she has been reported to have the face of a bat or a horse. Some believe that she is as likely to haunt forests and deserted roadways as she is the riverbanks. Still others have heard that her prey are not children but young men who have strayed from the straight and narrow. In an interesting blend of legends, she is sometimes described as a phantom hitchhiker who shares her woeful tale with whoever gives her a ride before vanishing from the vehicle.

Perhaps the most consistent element of La Llorona's story is the belief that she is to be feared. Even when she is not luring children to a watery grave or enticing young men to join her in death, the mournful phantom is considered to be a harbinger of doom. So beware the forlorn cries that carry through the stormy night. It may be the tortured wraith of La Llorona—a funereal figure no one wishes to encounter.

The Ghostly Music of the San Bernard River

Long ago, by the San Bernard River in Brazoria County, an old hermit fiddler was ruthlessly murdered by two pirates who had sought refuge inland as a storm raged along the Gulf of Mexico. Maybe. It might actually have been *two* fiddlers who froze to death beneath a tree on the riverbank. Or a musician who threw himself and his instrument into the water after finding his beautiful fiancée dead of a snake bite only hours before they were to be wed. Then again, the devastated lover may not have committed suicide, but instead moved to a lonely island in the river to spend the rest of his days making mournful music.

It is impossible to know with any certainty what happened. The stories are numerous and varied and shrouded in the mists of time. But, while the details of the actual tragedy are elusive, the resulting ghost story has become a well-known staple of Texas lore. For more than a century, people have reported hearing sweet, haunting, otherworldly melodies at Music Bend on the San Bernard River.

It is said to sound like a violin, a harp and even a human voice. It has been described paradoxically as the "sweetest and most terrible music" ever heard. It has been heard by many—both skeptics and believers—and their stories are intriguing.

One elderly gentleman lived for a time with a family whose home was near the river. All members of the family had heard the phantom music at one time or another;

they were all believers. The old fellow scoffed at them all. "It's nonsense," he insisted. To prove his point, he rowed his boat out over Music Bend day after day and returned each night to report that nothing out of the ordinary had happened. One evening, however, the old man was pale and shaken when he arrived back at the house. He told his hosts that he had been rowing over the Bend, as usual, when a deep chill swept over him. He felt every hair on his body stand on end. And then he heard the music: distant, sweet strains of a violin drew closer, filled the air and seemed to envelop him in the little boat. "I have heard it," he whispered, "and I never want to hear it again."

A similar sentiment was expressed back in 1920 by the members of a search party who retrieved the remains of two drowned girls from the San Bernard near Music Bend. As the men pulled the lifeless bodies up out of the murky water, music began to play. It was described as the most beautiful funeral music imaginable. That said, the searchers all admitted that they never again wanted to hear such harmonies.

On rare occasions, people have reported seeing apparitions near the haunted place on the river. In one case, a woman was one of a large number of people enjoying a midnight boating excursion when she saw something she could not explain. By the bright, full moon, she clearly saw a man on the shore, with a bridle over his arm. He moved down to the water's edge, then turned and went back into the woods. This may not have seemed strange, but for three things: the woman was able to see only the upper half of the man's body; he seemed to glide, rather than walk; and, despite her efforts to point the man out to her companions, the woman found that she was the only person on the boat able to see the stranger.

In another instance, a teenaged boy was horseback riding at night along a road just above the notorious Music Bend when he encountered a man and a woman sitting in the middle of his path. Their manner was extremely peculiar, and the boy's horse refused to advance on the couple. The horse's behavior, combined with the proximity to the famous haunted waters, was sufficient to convince the boy to find another route.

Perhaps these strange apparitions are somehow connected to the legend of the spectral melody. Or perhaps there is something in the geography of that small area that encourages ghostly manifestations of all kinds. That, along with the origin of the haunting music, appears destined to remain a mystery of the San Bernard River.

The Phantom Horseman of Chisholm Hollow

It is not unusual to hear of a ghost acting as an omen, such as the banshees and radiant boys of legend who prophesy death in the households where they appear. It *is* unusual to have a spirit forecast events on a much larger scale—except in the hills of central Texas, where there is a formidable apparition who does just that. He appears as a Spanish conquistador, clad in heavy armor and riding a powerful midnight black steed. Every time this fearsome rider has been seen in the little valley that is known as Chisholm Hollow, it has meant only one thing: the United States was about to enter into war.

In 1846, a rancher named McConnell became the first of many to witness the ghostly conquistador. McConnell had ventured into the valley while tracking a pack of wolves that had been tormenting his cattle. The rancher was so intent upon the task at hand that, at first, he barely heard the metallic clanking sound in the distance. It grew louder and nearer, though, causing McConnell to snap to attention. He looked up just in time to see the massive apparition of an armored rider and his thundering horse bearing down upon him.

Enormous hooves pounded the earth, and the heavy, rhythmic sound of iron striking iron could be heard as the rider's shield battered against his breastplate. The light of the setting sun reflected brightly off the soldier's gauntlets and helmet as he and his brawny steed passed the astonished rancher and roared off into the distance. McConnell gaped after the phantom and saw to his further amazement that the towering vision vanished abruptly before leaving the valley. The terrified fellow wasted no more time. He mounted his own rather small pony and urged it to run as quickly as possible in the direction of home.

McConnell had a dramatic tale to tell his friends. Nothing as exciting had ever happened in their rural part of the world. Unfortunately, the very next day, the rancher's experience was overshadowed by the onset of the Mexican War.

It was 15 years before the next recorded sighting of the phantom rider. The story had been all but forgotten when, on April 10, 1861, a man named Emmett Ringstaff saw the fearsome apparition thundering through the hollow. It was not long after that the country was plunged into civil war. When the Spanish-American War began just after the rider's next appearance—witnessed by Arch Clawson, Ed Shannon and Sam Bullock—people began to take note of the pattern.

In January 1917, the United States was once again on the brink of battle, but this was likely far from the minds of three young Texans who were spending one day deer hunting in the hills. They followed a trail into Chisholm Hollow, all the while laughing about the famous legend. When the phantom conquistador came charging out of the woods, however, the laughter stopped and the frantic scramble for safety began. The hunters then believed in the spectral horseman. Within a month, when American troops began to mobilize for the First World

War, the young men had also come to believe in the ghost's prophetic powers.

The last known sighting of the armored rider came on December 7, 1941. A group of people were traveling home from a prayer meeting that Sunday, on the road that ran through Chisholm Hollow. As the car passed the famous haunt, the driver brought it slowly to a stop. He told his passengers that he thought he heard the sound of a galloping horse. At that moment, the towering black animal and its armor-clad rider burst out of the woods and onto the road. The fearsome apparition paused for a moment beside the vehicle and its terrified occupants, then reared mightily and charged off into the trees. The church-goers knew the legend. They rushed home and turned on their radios. Bulletins were already being broadcast about the bombing of Pearl Harbor—the terrible event that would finally bring the United States into World War II.

It is interesting to note that the phantom rider was never seen prior to the American involvement in Korea and Vietnam. In his book *Ghosts Among Us* (Berkley Publishing Group, 1990), Brad Steiger suggested that the reason may have been that these conflicts were both officially described as "police actions." There was no actual declaration of war and, therefore, no war for the ghost to predict.

Steiger also relayed some interesting information regarding the possible identity of the horseman in Spanish-style armor: "a Spanish fort had been located near the hollow when Texas had been under Spain's control. According to the historians, the garrison that had been stationed near the fort had been massacred by Comanche Indians around 1700."

Could one of the murdered Spanish soldiers have become the phantom rider? It would require more documented sightings, with detailed descriptions of the horseman's attire, to venture an educated guess. But no one wishes for another spectral appearance—for when this ghost comes thundering through the hollow on his powerful horse, he brings with him the worst possible news. And no matter how dramatic and exciting it may be to witness a famous apparition, no ghost sighting is worth a war.

Lachusa

In May 2000, Efrain Yanez of Donna, Texas, wrote to *FATE* magazine about an unforgettable experience that he had when he was 10 years old and accompanied his truck-driver father on a trip to Laredo. The large cargo of melons was to be delivered before sunrise, so the two had been driving through the cool, early hours of the morning. Efrain recalled the pale glow of the moon lighting their way as the truck raced along at highway speed. The calm was soon to be interrupted.

"All of a sudden," wrote Efrain, "the passenger-side door opened where I was sitting. To my surprise, I saw an old lady standing on the side step, holding the door open and beckoning me with her finger to go with her."

The boy looked at his father. The elder Yanez simply

told his son, "Give me your hand, and close the door." He gave no indication that he had seen the old woman. Efrain looked to his right and found that he could no longer see her either. The door, however, remained wide open, despite the air pressure created by the truck's high speed. Efrain's father grasped his wrist, and the boy reached over and pulled the door shut.

Father and son rode in silence for some time. Finally, Efrain asked his father if he had seen the woman holding open the door. The man responded with a raised eyebrow and sideways glance, suggesting that he had not. Before Efrain could explain himself further, the crone suddenly appeared again—this time, in the middle of the road directly in front of the truck. Efrain's father had no time to react. There was a dull thud of impact before he managed to slam his foot down on the brake pedal. Once the truck had come to a stop, the shaken twosome climbed out to face the gruesome scene. What they discovered, according to Efrain Yanez, was a shock and a mystery: "There was no blood on the truck's grille, just white feathers from a large bird. My dad said that it was a *lachusa*—a 'witch owl' that people turn into."

Efrain Yanez's eerie tale might be a rare firsthand encounter with the gigantic, supernatural creature known as "Lachusa." The well-known Mexican-American legend of Lachusa tells of an enormous black bird with no feet that acts as a warning or omen and torments those who have committed terrible sins.

There are notable discrepancies between Yanez's story and the legend, but there are similarities as well. According to Rosemary Ellen Guiley in *Harper's Encyclopedia of*

Mystical and Paranormal Experience (Harper Collins, 1991), "Birds ... are the omens of death, especially black birds such as crows and nocturnal birds such as owls." With that taken into consideration, the huge black crow of legend and the sinister white "witch owl" of Efrain Yanez's story have much in common. Yanez himself wondered, "Was death calling me at a young age, or was it some message from the dead?"

It is a chilling question to which, several years later, there still remains no answer. The only one that truly knows why that frightening creature summoned Efrain Yanez on that dark early morning is the creature itself: Lachusa.

Here Stands Brit Bailey

In Brazoria County, in an area called Bailey's Prairie, there is a well-known phantom light. Some say the glowing, ghostly orb will appear on any given night. Others claim that the mysterious phenomenon takes place only every seventh year. Still others have suggested that the specter is an invisible rider on a horse who patrols the area constantly, but that his lantern can be seen only every seventh year. All sources agree on one point: the ghost of Bailey's Prairie is its namesake, James Briton Bailey.

Brit Bailey was a legendary Texas frontiersman who seemed determined to die as colorfully as he had lived. In his will, he stated that he was to be buried standing upright, with a gun over his shoulder and a full jug of whiskey by his feet. Brit explained that he had never looked up to any man in his lifetime and did not intend to change after death. He clearly had no intention of changing his epic drinking habit, either—but his widow had other ideas. Perhaps she felt that it would keep him from his final reward, or perhaps she simply believed that Brit had drunk more than his share before dying, but for some reason, the whiskey jug never made it into the old pioneer's grave. Some say that this is why the man has yet to rest.

The family who bought the late Brit Bailey's house and land had not been there long before they realized that Brit had not quite moved on. By the time they packed up and left, they swore they had seen the old man's ghostly figure drifting about the house on three occasions. Soon after, many people who traveled past Bailey's land at night

Famous frontiersman Brit Bailey requested that he be buried in a
standing position, so that no one could say, "Here Lies Brit Bailey..."

reported seeing a strange, shimmering globe or column
of light. There were those who tried to track the illumination to its source, but never with any luck. The apparition
was as elusive as it was fascinating.

The ghost light has been regularly seen over Bailey's
Prairie since the mid-1800s. It is famous now, a staple of
Texas ghost lore. If the light truly is a sign that Brit's ghost
is eternally searching for his brown jug, it may just stay
around forever. As no one knows the exact site of Brit
Bailey's unmarked grave, it would be difficult to give the
man his whiskey now.

The Ghosts of Love Gone Wrong

Lost love, unrequited love, eternal love, tragic love—these are the fodder of poems, songs and even ghost stories. When a relationship goes awry, the emotions involved are often strong enough to draw the longing lover's spirit back to the scene. Happily, there are also some tender stories of sweethearts who cannot be separated, even in death.

The following four tales are of Texans whose star-crossed romances appear to have affected them in an everlasting fashion.

☠

Don Ramos was a powerful, wealthy man. He owned huge herds of cattle and the vast territory of land upon which they roamed. He had a fine, big house and many servants in his employ. He was handsome, and he was unmarried, the most sought-after bachelor in all of South Texas. Many young women dreamed of becoming his wife, and one proud and arrogant girl in particular expected that she would. While she confidently waited for Don Ramos to ask for her hand in marriage, however, fate intervened. Ramos returned from a Mexican trip with a lovely bride named Leonora. The other woman, humiliated and devastated, secretly vowed revenge.

The newlywed couple lived happily for a time. Eventually, however, business called Don Ramos away to

Spain. It was to be a long journey, and the two parted tearfully, knowing that it would be many months before they could be together again. The separation was difficult for both the wealthy rancher and his lovely Leonora. But, when Don Ramos finally returned home, he found his bride waiting with wonderful news.

"We are to have a child," she told him, in their first moments alone. Don Ramos beamed with pride.

"I must tell everyone!" he announced. "I will have an heir!"

Sadly, the joyousness of the couple's reunion was short-lived. Don Ramos had been home for only a few days when poisonous rumors began to reach his ears. The child, it was whispered, was not his. Leonora had been unfaithful to Don Ramos in his absence.

The man flew into a great rage. Leonora wept and pleaded with her husband.

"I could never be untrue to you," she sobbed. "I love you!" The words were useless against the humiliation and pain that Ramos felt. His pride demanded that action be taken. He stormed out of the room, leaving Leonora wailing, and summoned a few of his most trusted men. When they had gathered, the infuriated Don Ramos assigned them a terrible deed.

"Have my wife dressed in black," he instructed, "then put her on a horse and take her one day's journey to the north. At sunset, you will hang her from the tallest tree you can find!"

If the men were horrified, they did not show it. After all, Don Ramos was their employer, and the master of his household. And if the rumors they had heard were true ...

But the rumors were not true. As tragedy played out in the Ramos home, the embittered woman who had expected to become Don Ramos's wife laughed secretly behind her hand. She had spread the seeds of gossip, seeing in those lies one final opportunity to get her man. She expected Leonora to be sent away. In fact, Leonora was being sent to her death.

All day, the terrified young wife and her escort of somber cowboys rode northward. She pleaded her innocence and begged for her life. She wept pitiably and screamed in rage. Finally, as the sun became low in the sky, and the men threw a length of heavy rope over a strong branch of the tallest tree in sight, Leonora grew quiet.

"You know this is a sin," she said, as they placed the noose around her neck. "I am innocent, and I will never let you forget this horrible crime you are about to commit." The only reply was a cracking whip which struck the rear quarters of Leonora's horse. The animal bolted, producing a rising cloud of dust with its hooves and leaving its rider swinging. Eventually, she became still, cutting a dark and ominous silhouette against the orange sunset sky.

If the jealous gossip sensed Leonora's death and felt any wicked pleasure from it, it was only for a moment. For the detestable woman would soon learn that, in destroying Don Ramos's marriage, she had also destroyed Don Ramos. As his wife and his cowboys rode north, Ramos had spent the day riding south. He, too, watched the shadows grow long, and as the sun touched the horizon, he drew his pistol. Within moments of the time the rope ended Leonora's life, a bullet ended the life of Don Ramos. The tragedy was complete—but the story was not, for Leonora was determined to keep her dying word: she would not let anyone forget.

Since her death, Leonora's mournful ghost is said to appear frequently. Passersby often report having seen a beautiful young woman, dressed in black, weeping at the side of the road. When a kind motorist stops to offer assistance, however, her form becomes as insubstantial as a puff of smoke, then disappears. This is believed to be Leonora, haunting the site of her death, which is now the intersection of highways 281 and 141, south of Alice. It has been more than 200 years, but this wronged young bride remains adamant. She "will never let you forget."

☠

Should you ever take an evening walk along the west bank of the San Gabriel River, near the little town of San Gabriel in Williamson County, pay close attention to the soft sounds you hear. It may be the breeze rustling leaves, it may be the river singing its liquid lullaby, or it may be two whispering lovers, long dead, who still meet at the water's edge.

Many decades ago, a beautiful young woman lived with her wealthy parents in their fine ranch house overlooking the river. The girl had everything that money could buy and the misfortune to desire the one thing she could never have—an open relationship with a handsome young Mexican ranch-hand. The two were deeply in love but knew their romance would meet with severe disapproval if ever it was discovered.

The lovers tried for a time to stay apart but found that their hearts could not bear it. And so, they devised a plan. Every evening at sundown, the girl would stroll along the west bank of the San Gabriel. The dashing cowboy would walk toward her, but on the east bank, so as not to arouse suspicion. They would meet at a location where a fallen log spanned the river, forming a foot bridge. The young man would nimbly walk across the gnarled tree trunk and into the waiting embrace of his darling. Each considered those stolen twilight moments, when they would walk arm and arm whispering endearments, to be the best of the day.

The lovers' ruse had one flaw which they were unable to overcome. If it rained, the girl could not leave her parents' house on the pretense of a pleasant stroll. When autumn came, and the rain persisted for several days, the sweethearts were forced to suffer a long separation in misery. On the day the sun finally broke through the clouds, the girl put on her most beautiful dress and ran down to the banks of the swollen river with an eager heart.

She hurried along the muddy path to the crude footbridge. There, approaching on the east bank, was her beloved. "My darling!" she cried and stretched her arms out to greet him. On the other side of the San Gabriel, the young man's eyes lit with joy at the sight of his dearest. He hopped up on the fallen log and began to run lightly across it. Unfortunately, days of torrential rain had left the surface slick and, at the midpoint, the handsome cowboy lost his footing and tumbled into the churning water. The girl screamed in horror as her young man was pulled under by the swiftly moving current and was swept downstream.

It was too much for the girl to bear. Insane with grief, she began to frantically pace the path, calling her lover's name. For hours she continued, until her voice grew hoarse and the moon had risen high in the sky. Eventually she was discovered, staring out over the raging water with vacant eyes.

It is said that she never fully regained her senses. On each evening of her remaining days, the young woman walked down to the banks of the San Gabriel and met a lover whom only she could see. Sometimes it seemed that she could also envision the terrible accident playing out before her yet again. On those occasions, she would scream out, reliving each moment of the horror and pain.

It surprised no one when the girl's body eventually succumbed to the illness of her mind. On her final day, as she lay on her deathbed, she made one request. "Should I live to see the sunset," she whispered, "take me down to the river path."

The girl's anguished parents were willing to do anything to make their daughter's last hours comfortable. When sunset came, they eased her onto a stretcher and carried her down to the San Gabriel River. As they approached the spot that had once been such a happy meeting place for her, a light came into her eyes. "Please—set me down here," she asked. Once on the ground, the girl summoned her final strength to raise herself on one elbow. The air seemed to shimmer above her, and an expression of pure happiness softened her face. "My love," she whispered, and then died.

Since that day, it is said that the footpath on the west bank of the river is haunted by the souls of those two lovers. Each sunset, they meet at their accustomed spot and walk along together, whispering sweet words. Though they could not share their lives, in death, they have found an eternity in which to be together.

☠

There is a mountain near a small West Texas village where mysterious, flickering lights are often seen. While skeptics insist that there must be some natural explanation for the phenomenon, there are others who know better. The lights are a sign, they say, that poor Dolores is still searching for her murdered lover.

The story began more than 100 years ago, with a young couple who were very much in love. Dolores was a sweet village girl, and Jose, a handsome shepherd. The two had plans to marry and raise a family. The only thing that kept them apart for any amount of time was Jose's work. He had been entrusted with the large herds of sheep that wandered in the canyons and as he cared for them, he frequently had to camp far from the village.

On the many nights when Jose was away, he and Dolores would signal their love to one another. When darkness fell, she would climb to the top of a small mountain near her home and light a fire. Out in the canyons, Jose would ignite an answering flame. Then each could sleep easily, knowing that all was well with the other.

One night, however, it became apparent that all was not well with Jose. Dolores sat on her mountaintop until she ran out of kindling with which to feed her fire. The last of the day's light had bled out of the sky, and still, there was no signal from Jose. Dolores returned to the village full of fear.

"Something has happened to Jose!" she told her father. "You must help him!"

All the villagers knew that Jose's job was one fraught with danger. In the canyons, a shepherd constantly ran the risk of running into warring Apaches. Jose's failure to signal Dolores was a real cause for concern, and a search party was quickly organized. Unfortunately, all the men were able to do was recover Jose's body, which had been shot, scalped and left on the canyon floor.

Dolores was heartbroken and became utterly despondent. She went about her daily routines but seemed joyless to all who met her. The villagers mourned for her as well as Jose but held out hope that she might one day begin to heal. That hope was dashed when, a short time after Jose's death, Dolores gathered her basket of kindling and climbed to the top of the mountain. Her concerned father followed her and found her standing by a small fire, staring out into the distant darkness.

"Come home, daughter," he begged, but Dolores would not budge. She stayed until the fire had burned down to ashes. She returned the next night, and the next night and the night after that. It became her melancholy ritual to climb the mountain every evening and light a signal that would never be answered. The good people of the village were saddened to watch Dolores grow old and gray this way, never recovering from her loss.

Eventually she passed away, but it is said that her ritual continues. In *Ghost Stories of Old Texas* (Eakin Press, 1983), Zinita Parsons Fowler wrote:

> although Dolores has now truly been dead for many years, it is said that on certain evenings, especially when nothing, not even the moon, lights the darkness, the flickering of her fire can be seen on top of the mountain ...

... others say that if you climb to the top of Dolores Mountain on the evening after the fire is seen, you will find ashes blown about by the constant West Texas wind, and perhaps a bit of brushwood, charred and darkened by the fire kept burning by a [young woman] whose love will never die.

☠

Her name was Francesca, and she was undeniably beautiful. He was called Ferenor, and he was a novice priest. When they met inside the walls of old Fort Stockton, both of their lives took a dramatic turn. They fell immediately in love, and all thoughts of taking his final vows left the young priest's mind.

One stormy night, the two decided that they could no longer wait to be together. Braving the violent wind and lashing rain, Francesca and Ferenor went to see the young man's uncle, who was the priest of the garrison church. They asked the padre to marry them, and he responded with outrage. The lovers pleaded their case passionately, but the old man would not listen. He turned them out into the tempest and slammed the door.

Ferenor tried to take Francesca home, but in the raging storm, he missed the trail to her family's house. When the young priest turned back to find it, he lost his sense of direction. The two wandered through the wilderness in the torrential rain until they were soaked through and freezing cold. Francesca was becoming weak with fatigue, and Ferenor began to feel hopeless. Then suddenly, there was something on the horizon.

"Francesca! Look! A light!"

Ferenor felt certain that he was looking at a glimmering lantern in the window of a settler's house. It was distant, but he knew that he could get there on his own. He settled his exhausted Francesca by a large rock, sheltering her from the storm as best he could. "Stay here, darling," he told her. "I'll be back soon, with help."

Ferenor walked toward the light for some time but grew concerned when it seemed that he was no nearer to it than he had been before starting out. As he paused to consider this, the light appeared to move, then vanished from sight, reappearing in a different location. *It is a trick of the storm,* Ferenor told himself, *an optical illusion.* But when the beacon disappeared for the fourth time, the devastated young man had to admit defeat. He was exhausted, hopelessly lost and becoming frantic about the condition of his beloved Francesca. "Francesca!" he called out. "Francesca!" The wind carried his words away but brought back no answer. Ferenor panicked and began to run. The ground was slippery with mud, and he fell twice. Each time, he scrambled back to his feet, desperate to reach his sweet Francesca. The third time Ferenor's feet slipped out from under him, his skull cracked against a flat rock. The world fell dark and silent for the young priest. He lay unconscious until it was nearly dawn.

When Ferenor awoke, the storm had subsided. The faint glow on the eastern horizon helped him to regain his sense of direction. But, although he searched the area thoroughly, he was never able to find his precious Francesca. Rumors eventually began to circulate that the girl had been seen living in camp with a roving band of Comanches. Some said that the Comanche chief, who had wanted Francesca to be his own bride, had lured the lovesick Ferenor into the wilderness with a torch.

Ever since, Brewster County has been haunted by a mysterious flickering light and Ferenor's tormented cry. "Francesca! Francesca!" can be heard on many cold, rainy nights—and is considered to be an omen of back luck. For when a lover sees the false beacon or hears the young priest's desperate call, it means that there is danger facing him or his beloved. It is an echo of the tragedy that separated Ferenor and Francesca so very long ago.

Legends of the Stampede

Writer Zinita Parsons Fowler once offered a vivid description of a stampede, calling it "the wild, unchecked, thundering flood of terrified cattle that destroy[s] every living thing in its path." Cattle stampedes were a real and persistent danger to ranch-hands, and at the same time symbolic of all in the West that was wild, powerful and unwilling to be truly tamed. It is little wonder that many stampede stories have found their way into the folklore, and ghost lore, of Texas.

One of the most detailed and fascinating accounts is about a piece of land known as "Stampede Mesa." It is a flat, grassy place overlooking the White River in Crosby County that offered trail drivers an ideal place to bed down a large herd at night. There was the river, where the cattle could drink their fill, and the 200-acre mesa top, which offered good grazing and a natural pen of sorts. The hundred-foot drop-off into the river canyon acted as a natural barrier, so night guard of the herd could be reduced by half.

It is said that in the fall of 1889, a trail boss and his cowboys planned to stop over at the mesa with the 1500 head of cattle they were driving. When they arrived, however, they found a small-time rancher already camped there, with about 40 scrawny steers of his own. Within minutes, the old fellow's few gaunt, bawling animals had become mixed in with the hundreds of new arrivals. The rancher flew into a rage and demanded that his cattle be cut out of the larger herd immediately. The trail boss and his hands were tired from a long day's ride, however, and

Since the late 1800s, cowboys have been careful to avoid overnighting their cattle on the haunted place known as "Stampede Mesa."

unwilling to take orders from an impertinent old rancher. "You'll get 'em back come sunrise," the boss said, and refused to hear another word on the subject. When the rancher persisted, he was shown the barrel of a pistol. Humiliated, intimidated and outnumbered, the old man sulked off as the cowboys prepared to bed down.

It was a peaceful, moonless night, and the herd settled easily. The quiet was short-lived, however, because close to midnight, the cattle roared into a dreaded stampede. Something spooked them from the north, so they fled south, throwing themselves over the steep bluff and into the canyon. Two of the cowboys who tried to save them were swept along to meet the same fate. All but 300 head fell to their deaths, and the hands who had survived the stampede made a grim accusation. It was the old rancher, they said. They had seen him, waving a blanket and whooping, on the north side of the mesa.

"Get 'im," said the trail boss. "Bring 'im here alive, and bring that skinny horse of his, too."

The cowboys carried out their orders. The rancher was tracked down and hauled back to the top of the mesa. The trail boss then instructed his men to gag and blindfold the murderer and to tie him to his horse. The horse was then blindfolded as well and driven off the cliff. The trail riders left the old man's body to rot with the dead steers, in the canyon, and told themselves that justice had been done. The ghost of the rancher, however, seemed less willing to put the ugliness behind him.

It was not long before rumors about the mesa began to circulate. The location, which had long been considered the ideal place to hold a herd, was quickly gaining a bad reputation. Many trail riders reported having problems there with the cattle. The animals would become skittish for no particular reason. On a few occasions, stampedes started mysteriously, and disaster was averted only because of some quick action on the part of the ranch-hands. One or two men, their tongues loosened with liquor, claimed to have seen an eerie specter of a blindfolded man atop a horse, charging at their herd. Some spoke of seeing ghostly steers among their own cattle. And even the most level-headed and unflappable cowboys were willing to admit that there was a strange, unexplainable and undeniably bad feeling out there. Before long, it gained the name of "Stampede Mesa" and became known as a place to avoid.

☠

Of course, cattle are not the only animals known to stampede. Two other Texas legends exist, one involving phantom horses, and the other a mythical herd of albino buffalo.

The horses are said to appear in the Palo Duro Canyon on brightly moonlit nights. Those who have witnessed the phenomenon say it begins with a distant noise that grows nearer and swells into the clearly identifiable thunder of hooves. At some point, the specters appear—beautiful, translucent animals, galloping at full speed along the edge of the canyon. Both the image and the sound are said to vanish quite abruptly, leaving nothing but a chilling silence. Some believe that these are the ghosts of horses once massacred by soldiers in an effort to disable a number of Plains Indians tribes.

The mighty albino buffalo is a legend that grew among the people of one of those tribes: the Kiowa. Angered at the careless way white hunters had devastated the large herds of buffalo that once roamed across the Panhandle, the Kiowa began to speak of the animal's ultimate revenge.

According to the story, a herd of gigantic albino buffalo, growing stronger and larger every year, is hidden in underground caverns. It is foretold that when their numbers reach 60 million, they will emerge from their lair and stampede across the plains, destroying everything in their wake. On that day, it is predicted that the Kiowa nation will rise again, reclaiming all that they have lost.

The Murder Brand

Near the end of the 1800s, in the Big Bend country of Texas, a murder resulted in one of the strangest ghost stories ever told.

Ranchers in that vast, largely unfenced, territory were accustomed to having their cattle occasionally mix together. Strays were common, and ownership of each animal was a matter to be sorted out at round-up time. The issue became complicated only when the stray in question was an unbranded yearling.

In one such instance, a rancher named Henry Powe was coaxing an unmarked calf into his own herd during the round-up. A cowboy named Fine Gilliland took exception to the man's gall.

"I believe that animal's ours," bellowed Gilliland over the din of bawling cattle. Powe ignored the statement and carried on about his business. Gilliland, unwilling to let the matter rest, attempted to lasso the calf in question. That's when Powe decided to end the argument. He drew his pistol and fired a shot at the calf. The bullet missed its mark which, ultimately, caused much greater harm—for Gilliland thought that the gun had been aimed at him and drew his own six-shooter to fire in return. Gilliland turned out to be the better shot. Powe fell dead from his horse, and Fine Gilliland was forced to "hit the outlaw trail." He was eventually killed in a shoot-out with some Texas Rangers, but there still remained the matter of what to do about the calf.

Because of what had happened, there was no rancher who wanted the unlucky yearling. Instead, they burned it with a brand that would forever remind them of the terrible incident and turned the animal loose on the plains. It grew into a wild thing, spotted every so often by some cowboy. The bull's appearance would give a person chills, for the tall letters that had been seared into the hide of its flank spelled the word "MURDER."

Years went by, and the bull with the "murder" brand continued to appear. Eventually, there had been too many years, and people began to conclude that it was not the actual animal, but its ghost, that still roamed the plains. Even now, on occasion, there are whispered reports of a hulking gray bull that has been glimpsed on the horizon. There can be no mistake in identifying it, for only one such beast has ever worn its particular ominous brand.

El Muerto

His name was Vidal, and he was a Mexican bandit who plagued the ranchers of southern Texas by stealing their cattle. His crime spree came to an end when a band of vigilantes caught up with him and measured out a bit of Wild West justice. Vidal was beheaded by the cowboys. Whipped into a state of high emotion, however, the men did not stop at that. They thought it would be a good idea to securely strap Vidal's body onto the saddle of his horse and hang his sombrero-clad head from the saddle horn by a rawhide strap. They then set the poor horse loose, dooming it to wander aimlessly about with its gruesome burden.

Every so often, some traveler would encounter the horse and its macabre rider. Terrified, the person would shoot at the headless monster. Often, they knew that their bullets had struck the mark but, still, the horseman did not topple. Stories were told and, eventually, the headless rider known as *El Muerto* became legendary.

After a very long time, Vidal's horse was finally captured, and the corpse removed from its back. The dead bandit was buried near Ben Bolt—but sightings of the headless one did not end. It is said that the ghostly image of a horse and its headless rider are sometimes seen around the Coastal Plains. It is *El Muerto*, seemingly intent upon perpetuating the eerie illusion that he will not die.

Texas Treasure

Texas folklore abounds with tales of buried treasure, unmarked mines and the spectral keepers of these legendary lost fortunes. Pirates and smugglers who found haven in the Gulf of Mexico and its tributaries are said to have left behind untold riches buried in the soil. Legendary veins of gold and silver, fabled to lie beneath the great state, are believed by some to have been mined briefly, then hidden and forgotten. There is apparently a lot of loot to be found in Texas—if one knows where to look. The inconvenient absence of accurate treasure maps leaves the hunter with only two options: a state-of-the-art metal detector, or a message from a ghostly guardian of the booty. Fortunately, there seem to be many such specters to be found. Here are but a few ...

☠

The banks of the San Gabriel River near Thorndale are haunted by a spirit that appears as an incandescent, yellow light that roams between the river and the site of a cabin that once belonged to an old settler. The ghostly light is said to be the settler himself, a bachelor named Snively, who is guarding a cache of gold that was never even his.

Legend has it that the treasure was stolen and ended up in the hands of a group of outlaws planning to take it across the Mexican border. When the thieves began to suspect that they were being followed by Texas Rangers, they decided that it would be safer to bury the contraband and return for it later. They chose a piece of ground near old Snively's cabin and then decided that old Snively himself should be a part of the plan.

In those ruthless days, it was common practice to place a dead body a few feet above a stash of buried treasure. The logic may have been that anyone snooping around the freshly turned earth would find the corpse and assume it was a grave—or it may have been that the phantom of the dead person was believed to stand guard over the wealth that lay beneath his remains. The outlaws likely held the latter belief, for when they captured old Snively, it is said that they made him swear to protect their gold. Snively took an oath, fearfully stammering out the last words he would ever utter. The merciless bandits murdered the man in cold blood and buried his body with the treasure. They then headed for the border, planning to return when the heat had died down. Perhaps it never did, or perhaps the criminals themselves did not live to see the day—but, for whatever reason, no one ever came back for the loot.

It wasn't long after that Snively's neighbors began to notice the glowing, yellow orb that traveled to and from the riverbank. It was particularly apt to appear on dull, rainy nights. After a time, a few of the more curious and brave folks tried to follow the light to its source, but each attempt resulted in the tracker becoming disoriented and lost. When rumors began to be whispered about the buried bounty, the greedy lined up to see the light and search for the treasure. Only one fellow ever claimed to find the site, but the San Gabriel flooded its banks, sweeping landmarks away before he had the chance to dig.

It would seem that no matter how brutally Snively was treated by the thieves, he took his oath to them very seriously. Good to his word, the gold remains well-guarded and untouched, somewhere on the banks of the San Gabriel River.

☠

Also in the Thorndale area, there is believed to be a hidden cache of wealth guarded by a spectral hound. In this case, a man named Pope was murdered for the gold he was known to have sequestered away near his little cabin. Unfortunately for the murderer, the gold was hidden so well that it could not be found. Only Pope knew its whereabouts, and he was dead. The villain, no doubt cursing his lack of foresight, was forced to leave without his reward.

After the killing, people noticed a strange stray dog wandering about near Pope's shack. Other animals shied away from the dog, and it soon became apparent why. The dog was a phantom: people would try to touch it only to have the apparition vanish before their eyes. Stones were thrown at the beast, and bullets fired upon it, to no effect. Eventually, people came to assume that the eerie mongrel was the ghost of Pope, standing guard over his fortune.

☠

The oil fields of Winkler County in West Texas contain one of the most unexpected ghostly images one will ever encounter. Appearing as out of place as he is out of time is the specter of a Russian Cossack named Nicholi. Said to be a count who escaped the Russian Revolution, Nicholi moved to Texas and became involved in the oil industry. While the young blueblood learned the business by working in the field, he kept his fortune hidden away in a coyote den, safe until the day he felt ready to invest it.

There were others who did not share Nicholi's cautious and systematic approach to business. They were thieves who planned to come upon wealth in a speedier fashion by stealing what the young Russian had. The men kidnapped Nicholi and demanded to know where his money was hidden. "I would rather die than tell you," he said. And then, he did.

After his death, Nicholi's ghostly image began to wander around the oil derricks and fields near Wink, Texas. He has even appeared in the small town, a gauzy figure wandering down Hendricks Boulevard.

On a dirt road east of Wink, in 1950, Nicholi's spirit was witnessed by someone who was destined to become a legend in his own right: Roy Orbison. Orbison may have been very close to the Cossack's hidden fortune at the time of the sighting. Nicholi is believed to have concealed his wealth between three and five miles due east of Wink.

☠

Somewhere in Leon County is a little piece of land once owned by an ex-Confederate soldier who missed his chance at wealth.

The man bought the property after the Civil War and settled there to farm it with his family. One night the man had a vision. He saw a strange-looking woman in unusual attire walk through his front gate and cross the yard. The usually fierce guard dogs didn't even acknowledge her presence. The woman approached the fellow and spoke clearly to him. "Dig in your little pasture and you will find treasure," she said.

The man dismissed what he had seen as a strange dream, but the apparition seemed unwilling to give up. A few nights later, she came to him again and was more specific in her instructions. "Dig in your little pasture," she implored. "Dig beneath the white rose." That was more intriguing, as the drought-stricken pasture had little growing in it.

The next day, the man and his wife decided to go on a treasure hunt. Indeed, they discovered a scrawny little bush supporting two wilted, white blossoms. The excited couple began to dig. When they had gone no more than two feet down, however, the shovel struck a large, heavy stone. That was all the discouragement the man required. He gave up and put his shovel away.

The wife remained curious about the visions, however, and told the story to a few trusted friends. Before long, word got out, and the husband became the butt of many jokes. A short time later, when the man's brother-in-law offered him a handsome sum for the farm, he eagerly took it and was glad to be disassociated with the source of his embarrassment. Later on that year, though, when the fellow noticed his brother-in-law had plowed the pasture and was suddenly spending lavishly, he wondered if he had done the right thing.

Mary A. Sutherland, the woman who recounted the story for inclusion in the 1924 volume *Legends of Texas* (Folklore Associates, Inc.), closed with an editorial comment:

It only remains to be said that, though a fine man, Mr. H—, the teller of this story, was the kind of man who would miss a chance at wealth rather than incur the ridicule of neighbors or exert himself in raising a stone.

The Palo Duro Canyon, home to the ghosts of horses slaughtered by the cavalry ("Legends of the Stampede," page 169), is also the scenic location of legendary lost gold.

The story tells of a small group of Mexican bandits who made off with a bank payroll and escaped into the canyon. The thieves were captured within days, but were no longer carrying the stolen gold coins. Eventually, the men admitted to having buried the wealth. "It is in the canyon," they said, "near a rock that looks like a lighthouse."

There is a rock formation in Palo Duro called "The Lighthouse" because of the way it towers over the rest of the canyon. This prominent landmark is frequently visited and photographed but, to date, it has not provided any visiting tourist with a cache of gold. That can mean one of two things: either the legend is fiction, or the treasure is still out there.

Four hundred years ago, it is said that Spanish padres from the Paso del Norte Mission mined a rich vein of gold in the mountains west of El Paso. For decades, they worked undisturbed. Then, in 1680, their safety was threatened when the Pueblo Indians of New Mexico revolted. The Indians had begun to kill or drive off all Spaniards in their wake, and the padres, fearing for their lives, decided to flee. Before doing so, they took all the valuables from the Mission, hid them in the shaft of the gold mine and cleverly concealed its entrance. Then, with the property of the church safely stowed away, the priests were able to concentrate on preserving their own lives.

Sadly, many lives were lost during that terrible time. After a while, there was no one remaining from the Paso del Norte Mission who recalled where the entrance to the mine was actually located. Those who perished seem to remember, though. Some people who have searched the area for the "Lost Padre Mine" have encountered the ghosts of priests who once worked there. Others claim that on certain nights, one can see flickering lights on the mountainside—the luminescent, spectral memory of fires lit hundreds of years ago in the camps of the Spanish miners.

☠

Bill Sutton was a goat herder who had a farm south of Victoria in the mid-1800s. He was unpleasant, unsociable and perhaps the most miserly man in the county. Also, people dreaded having to do business with "Old Man Sutton," as he was more apt to settle financial disagreements with a pistol than with words.

Sutton eventually shot at the wrong man and wound up dead as a result. No one was sorry that the old crank was gone, but people were somewhat curious about his wealth. Bill Sutton had no friends and no heirs, and he had made a great deal of money and spent little. Some folks claimed that he had buried his fortune in little parcels among the huge oak trees that stood in a grove on his property. If there were any who tried searching for it, however, they would have been quickly discouraged.

Immediately following the mean old man's demise, Sutton's Mott, as the cluster of oaks was called, came to be known as haunted. It was no tame spiritual activity that took place there, either—people experienced terrifying events. Some people reported the grotesque vision of life-less bodies suspended by chains from the branches of the trees. Others witnessed hideous, malformed creatures dart-ing in and about the grove. Horses and dogs suffered terrible fright when required to travel past the Mott. Going through it was simply out of the question.

Over the many years there have undoubtedly been some brave enough, or foolish enough, to actually dig for the cache in Sutton's Mott. None have found it, though, so somewhere among the roots of those huge trees, the money remains for the taking. But treasure hunters should be fore-warned: it will not be an easy score. As nasty in death as he was in life, Bill Sutton clearly has no intention of giving away his gold.

☠

One of the most famous figures in Texas history and folklore is the pirate Jean Laffite. The French-born thief of the high seas gave up a profitable slave trade in New Orleans to form a pirate colony on Galveston Island in 1817. He ruled over his band of miscreants and took full advantage of his location by plundering ships of all nations in the Gulf of Mexico. Laffite erred in judgment by stealing from a few too many American vessels, however, and the U.S. Navy set out to oust the pirate and his crew from the island. The outlaws fled on Laffite's flagship, *The Pride*, and somehow managed to maneuver through the American and British blockade. But whoever said "you can't take it with you" could have been talking about the pirate and his treasure. Jean Laffite was said to have left countless chests of treasure buried along the Texas coastline, to which he was never able to return.

By some accounts, there are still tens of millions of dollars worth of gold secreted away beneath the shifting sands of several islands and along the coastal area from Mexico to Louisiana. The idea of such riches would turn many ordinary people into eager treasure hunters, desperately seeking maps where "X marks the spot." But here's a word to the wise: determining the exact locations is only half the challenge. The other half is getting past Laffite and his loyal gang of sentries. Though long dead, these notorious pirates are still jealously guarding their stashes of ill-gotten goods.

One of Jean Laffite's treasure troves is said to be near the place where the Neches River connects with Lake Sabine. Several years ago, a man acquired what seemed to be an authentic pirate's map marking this particular location. He followed it to the marshy ground near the banks of the Neches and began to dig in the spot where the gold was supposed to be. The man managed to remove only a few shovelfuls of earth, however, before he felt a shockingly cold force envelop him. The terrified man dropped his tools and ran, but not soon enough to save himself. The fellow's fright had been so great, he died of a heart attack only a few days later. The map was then obtained by two other men who were unwilling to heed that fatal warning. They dug in the same location. The twosome managed to escape with their lives but later claimed to have seen "hell and all its horrors." Despite their considerable trouble, the men emerged from their experience none the richer.

That invisible force could have been the wraith of any member of Laffite's murderous crew, but there have also been several ghostly appearances by the famous pirate himself. One took place in an old vacant house near LaPorte, where a weary Civil War soldier had sought shelter for the night. The man was awakened at midnight by a ghostly pirate with a fierce gaze who claimed to be the spirit of Jean Laffite. Laffite warned the terrified soldier that he was prepared to deal harshly with anyone who attempted to steal the treasure that was buried beneath the floorboards of the old house.

"I assure you," the fellow stammered, "I have no interest in your treasure. I only wanted a place to rest."

"Then I will leave you be," said Laffite. The apparition faded into the wall. The soldier, quite shaken and aware that he would never be able to go back to sleep, quickly gathered his belongings and left.

LaPorte may be where Jean Laffite's spirit makes his home, for there have been other ghostly sightings of the famous pirate in that area. Some people have awakened in the middle of the night to see Laffite's ghost, flamboyantly dressed in a red coat, standing by the bed. Others, who were actively searching for Laffite's personal treasure near LaPorte, have told of being choked and threatened by the furious specter of the pirate. At the University of Texas

Medical Branch in Galveston, however, many people have been convinced that Laffite remains on the island where he once led his criminal gang. On the exterior wall of the University's Ewing Hall, facing the bay, the likeness of a face has been mysteriously superimposed over the simple, gray concrete. History buffs claim that it is the image of Laffite—watching over his island and the treasure to which he can never return.

Chapter 6

Haunted Houses

✠

They say that home is where the haunt—that is, "heart"—is. Given our profound attachments to the places in which we live, it is no wonder that so many spirits choose to return home after they die. The problem is that most ghosts are insensitive to the fact that what was once their home has now become someone else's castle. And when the living and the disembodied vie for the same living quarters, the resulting feud is often dramatic.

Even those who don't believe in spirits will speak of houses having a good or bad "vibe." If the very walls of a building can be imprinted with emotions and memories, is it such a stretch of imagination to think that departed residents themselves might stay on? In the following tales of Texas houses, it would appear that they have.

✠

A Difficult Sale

The Highland Park home was a spacious two-story, built in the early 1900s. It was also vacant and had been on the market for a long time. At $20,000 below market value, the place was a bargain, yet it seemed somehow to put people off. Even the real estate agent who was trying so hard to sell the property had to admit that it gave her "a peculiar feeling." The agent's mother, who had one day visited the house with her daughter, concurred. The back bedroom on the second floor seemed particularly uncomfortable to her. She left it, shivering, and stated emphatically, "I do not like that room or this house."

Several days later, the real estate agent was hosting a party. Among the 20 guests was a psychic who seemed very interested in the story of the unsalable property. At his suggestion, the group spontaneously left their cocktails and hors d'oeuvres and paid a visit to the vacant house. What happened there was documented in the *Dallas Morning News*, November 30, 1975.

Although nobody had lived in the house for a year, "when [the group] walked in, [they] could smell stale tobacco smoke," reported the psychic. The man followed his impressions to the back bedroom on the second floor. The party-goers followed, and all 20 people then stood in a circle, holding hands. The psychic asked if anyone else was present.

The real estate agent later told the *News*, "all of a sudden, this whitish-gray mist appeared in the center of the room. It started low, went higher, and developed into an apparition of a young girl." The agent said that she could see through the figure to people on the other side of the circle. At one point, she stepped forward and watched her arm go right through the image. When she stepped back, the ghost was still there. "I tried to talk to her," the agent said, "[but] I couldn't get answers." After what "seemed like an eternity, the spirit began to move her arms, and disappeared from the head down." After the wraith vanished, the room was filled with the stench of tobacco. Nobody present had been smoking.

Later, the real estate agent surveyed her guests and determined that approximately half of those who had been in the room had seen the vision of the young girl. No one could offer an explanation. According to the *News*, the "windows in the room were covered ... [eliminating] any possibility that the apparition was a reflection from outside." The group could only conclude that they had witnessed an actual ghost and wondered who the girl might have been.

According to one report, a man had killed his own daughter in the house. The real estate agent said that an old trunk found in the attic contained several locks of a child's hair and a portrait of an elderly man. In the end, there was no way to know for sure what had taken place in the home. Only the result was obvious. Said the real estate agent: "It is not a happy house."

Eventually, the place sold for $30,000 below list price, or roughly half the market value. Did the buyers get a bargain? That really depends—upon how sensitive they were to the spirit world and how well they tolerated the smell of tobacco.

Ignoring Adelaide

In 1981, Mr. and Mrs. O.S. Bradley bought an exquisite Greek Revival house in Lampasas, Texas. Though it would take time, and money, to restore the nearly 100-year-old home, the Bradleys were pleased to take on the project.

As the couple researched the history of the home, one past resident stood out to them. Her name was Adelaide Higdon, and she had lived in the house for 56 years. Mrs. Bradley eventually told a reporter from the *Killeen Daily Herald*, "I thought of Adelaide so much, I confided in her as we began the changes." Adelaide seemed to be paying attention to those confidences, for the Bradleys soon began to sense that they were not alone in their home.

Adelaide did not appear outright to Mr. and Mrs. Bradley, nor did she whisper ghostly messages or play spooky pranks. The former lady of the house preferred to make her presence known through a powerful aroma. Every Friday evening, the pungent smell of frying liver and onions—known to be one of Adelaide's favorite dishes—would waft through the rooms.

The Bradleys were not particularly bothered by the phantom cooking until they began to talk to their neighbors. People who had known Adelaide Higdon and her husband began to tell the Bradleys disturbing stories, forcing them to wonder what sort of spirit they had made welcome in their home. When Mrs. Bradley discovered that Adelaide "was considered to be a very mean woman," she said that she simply "quit talking to her."

The snub seemed to work. Adelaide's ghost apparently left in a huff and took her favorite food with her. It wasn't long before the Bradleys no longer spent their Friday evenings smothered by the smell of fried liver and onions.

She's He-ere!

In the 1982 movie *Poltergeist*, a suburban family's world is turned upside down when a malevolent force takes up residence in their television set. A Plano woman named Carol Woods experienced a similarly possessed TV, but the spirit was friendly. In fact, she recognized it as her recently deceased grandmother.

Perhaps it had something to do with the fact that the woman was laid to rest on Friday the 13th, for the ghostly pranks started almost immediately.

"All of a sudden, the TV went haywire," Carol told a reporter for the *Dallas Times Herald*. "It would change channels, adjust the volume very high, and turn itself on in the middle of the night."

It was a new television, still under warranty. A repairman was called to the house twice, but the supernatural set continued to act up. That is, until Carol's grandmother became bored with it and decided to change venues.

"Finally, the TV settled down and Grandmother took up residence in the smoke alarm, making it beep all of the time," laughed Carol, adding, "It's just the kind of thing she would do."

The smoke detector was not the playful spirit's last stop.

After a while, Carol began to sense her grandmother's presence in the upstairs bathroom. At that point, she began to communicate with the ghost.

"I started talking to her, asking specific questions," Carol told the *Times Herald*. The answers, she explained, would pop into her head. It was a nice opportunity for Carol to get to know her grandmother a little better—but it would seem that even spirits can be touchy about certain subjects. When Carol asked her grandmother about a child she had had late in life, who supposedly died, "she got mad and left for good."

Well, not quite for good. Carol did report that she sensed her grandmother's return some time later. "Sometimes I feel very watched over," she said.

It's probably a warm and comfortable feeling—as long as the appliances are working alright.

The House on Prairie Avenue

Leo Furrh took one look at the worn, old house on Prairie Avenue in Dallas and decided it was a good investment. He could renovate it. He could divide it into a duplex. It had old woodwork and a gabled roof and was not without charm. It was also not without a ghost, but Leo didn't discover that feature until after the sale had gone through.

When renovations were underway, the paranormal truth became apparent. Leo's son, Neil, was one of the first to notice. He was working on the exterior of the house one day, standing on a ladder by one of the second-floor windows. Suddenly, a face appeared, staring out at him from behind the glass. Neil was startled, as he had thought he was alone. He was even more shocked when he searched the house and found it to be empty.

Leo first encountered the specter when he was working in the house with his son-in-law. The two men were unnerved to hear the distinct sound of someone running up and down the stairs, when they could clearly see that no one was there. Leo Furrh described the incident in the October 30, 1972, edition of the *Dallas Times Herald*. "They'd always miss the bottom step," he said, "and give a sort of jump at the end."

Leo's son-in-law became quite interested in the strange phenomena and began to read books on the subject. Eventually, he convinced Leo to spend a night with him in the old house. The familiar sounds were heard on the staircase and, as usual, no living culprit could be found. On another night's visit, Leo had his first look at the ghost.

"I woke up and this woman was looking at me," Leo told the reporter. "She was dark-haired and about 35. She vanished—and reappeared in a few minutes near the doorway. Things have happened that you just can't explain."

Despite the strange occurrences, Leo Furrh stuck to his game plan. The house was renovated into a duplex, then offered for rent. But Leo realized what a poor investment the property was when he discovered that tenants were quickly frightened away.

"You can't get anyone to live in this place for long," he lamented. One of the first families to live there complained of hearing the spectral footsteps day and night and said that their teenaged son had been frightened by the appearance of a mysterious woman. They put double locks on the doors, hung crosses around the duplex and kept the lights on throughout the night. They even tore away strips of wood paneling, thinking that the ghost might have been the result of a body unceremoniously deposited there. Eventually, they just left. But Leo Furrh had been given an idea.

Perhaps discovering the identity of the ghost would help put it to rest, he thought. Leo found some spiritualists who were willing to visit the house and record their impressions. One was able to tell him that a tragedy had taken place in the home but could not be more specific than that. Leo then went to visit the previous owner, who was somewhat evasive. The only thing that Leo felt certain of was that the man had definitely known he was selling a haunted house. "He didn't seem surprised when I told him," Leo said. "He knew, alright."

Ultimately, Leo decided that selling the property himself was the last available option. At the time he spoke to the *Times Herald*, the house was sitting empty and on the market. As he waited for a prospective buyer, Leo did have to admit to one advantage of having a resident ghost.

"I don't worry about break-ins," he said. "I never lock the place. If someone comes in, he won't stay long ... "

The Old House

Most people who live in haunted houses are aware that the houses are haunted, as are any people in whom they have confided. Occasionally, a house will gain a "reputation," and stories about it—composed usually of skeletal facts and a huge, fleshy body of embellishment—will spread throughout a community. In some rare cases, a haunted house will become famous. The following tale has been passed from one generation to the next for a century now and shows every intention of being carried on. It is the story of an abandoned farmhouse, about three miles from Carrollton, and the eerie family that once lived there.

According to Zinita Parsons Fowler's 1983 book, *Ghost Stories of Old Texas* (Eakin Press), it was an old house and had been empty for some time. When word spread that a family had moved into the place, the people of the community were happy to hear it. A small group of well-wishers went out to welcome their new neighbors, taking a few groceries as gifts.

The kind people ended up feeling that their gesture was less than appreciated. The mother, father and three children they found living in the house were unfriendly and uncommunicative. The visit was brief and silent, and the only information the group gathered about the family was learned from what they saw.

They were poor—that was obvious. The clothing they wore was held together with patches upon patches, all worn and faded. They were thin as scarecrows, and the children's eyes were haunted by black circles. The house itself seemed to contain nothing but the bare essentials; there was no attempt at decoration and no suggestion of comfort. It was difficult to not pity the family despite the rude reception.

After several days, the local preacher decided that he would ride out to the house and extend a welcome on behalf of his congregation. He introduced himself to the cheerless husband and wife and was invited in for tea. For the remainder of the visit, the family sat in stony silence. The preacher's discomfort was overshadowed by his concern, however. The children appeared so undernourished, and the old home was so barren. For days after, he fretted over how to address this case of obvious need in a family that was so intensely private. Finally, he decided that another visit was in order. Perhaps he could coax a bit of conversation out of the people and learn more about their situation.

The preacher rode back out to the farmhouse one afternoon, only to find that no one was home. Certain that they would return soon, he made himself comfortable in the shade of a nearby tree. The preacher was so comfortable, in

The rural roads of Texas often lead to mystery—for there are many haunted houses to be found out in the country.

fact, that he soon dozed off to sleep. When he awoke, the hour had grown late, and there was still no sign of the family.

The preacher got up, stretched, and wandered around the scrubby farmyard. The family's decrepit wagon still sat by the barn, so surely they could not have gone far. The preacher decided to try knocking on the back door of the shack. When his knuckles touched the wood, the old door swung open. He decided to step inside.

"Hello?"

The word sounded hollow in the near-empty rooms. The preacher walked a little farther into the house and called out again. There was no answer. It was then that he noticed the old, stained kitchen table. It had been set for a meal, and meager servings of plain food sat on each of the five chipped dinner plates. None of it had been touched, though, and a few flies buzzed lazily over the bits of potato and slices of greasy meat. The preacher could smell that the food was beginning to turn. It had been out for some time. Suddenly, he was very concerned for the safety of these poor, quiet people. Then, as he turned to leave the house, he grew concerned for his own safety.

The fine hairs on the back of his neck stood up, and the preacher could feel eyes upon him. The sensation of being watched was overwhelming, and the man hurried to leave the house. Within moments, he was on his horse and off the property.

The preacher could not banish his concern for the family and eventually organized a search party. No clue was ever found, however. Finally, the abandoned building was struck by lightning and burned to the ground. It seemed to be the end of the story. But, of course, it was not.

Some time later, a traveling salesman was driving past the charred remains of the old house at sundown. He thought he heard something and stopped his horse so that he could listen more carefully. There it was—the sorrowful sound of a child, crying. The man squinted in the fading light and was able to make out the shape of a young boy, standing in the clearing. The child looked thin, forlorn, and lost.

"Little fella, you need some help?" the man called. He received no response but, suddenly, there were two older children standing beside the first youngster.

"They was all skin and bones," the salesman would later say, "and dressed in rags, to boot." He wanted to help them, and called out several times. The children simply stood and stared, though. They could not be coaxed into the comfortable wagon.

The sky was growing more dim by the minute, and suddenly the man felt a chill. He was being watched—he was certain of it. There was something or someone in the bushes, observing him, advancing on him .... The man turned away from the children, snapped his reins, and hurried into Carrollton. Three lonely forms stood in silhouette against the evening sky, watching him go.

The salesman made it safely to town, where he told a number of people about his creepy encounter. His honesty seemed to encourage others to come forward and report similar experiences by the old, burned-out shack. Soon everyone knew that it was a site to avoid and be wary of.

Some say it still is. When the wind is calm and the daylight is fading from the sky, be careful on the quiet back roads near Carrollton. Along one of them, you may find three crying children, dressed in rags, drawing your sympathy. And then, when you are suitably distracted, drawn some distance away from the safety of your vehicle, you will feel the eyes upon you ...

Have Ghost, Will Travel

Do ghosts haunt houses or the people who live in them? One story, originally told in the August 12, 1968, *Dallas Times Herald*, would lead you to wonder.

Four young women rented a house together in the mid-1960s. They hadn't been there long when strange things began to happen. Late at night, they were awakened by the sound of pebbles hitting their windowpanes. Lights would flash on and off in various rooms of the house, and personal belongings were frequently misplaced and then found in unlikely locations. Was someone playing a prank? Did the house have faulty wiring? The women were fairly sensible types who looked at all the reasonable explanations first. Eventually, however, they were forced to conclude that their house was haunted.

One of the oddest manifestations of this particular ghost was an assortment of aromas. Frequently, the roommates would be overwhelmed by the powerful scent of flowers, incense, vanilla or chocolate. When they began to also hear mysterious footsteps, they came to suspect that there were two separate spirits in the house. One would tread quite lightly, while the other had a heavy gait.

Only one of the ghosts ever showed itself. The first sighting took place one night when three of the friends went out, and the fourth elected to stay home. The three returned to the house and, through a window, noticed a girl in a pink sweater and black pants. Thinking that their roommate was still up, they chose to knock on the door instead of search through their purses for keys in the dark. When their friend opened the door, however, she was sleepy-eyed and clad in pyjamas. All four searched the house from top to bottom but, in the end, had to conclude that they had just seen one of their spectral housemates. The apparition—a dark, slender woman in her early thirties—was to be seen several more times. Interestingly, while her features always remained the same, her wardrobe often changed. The roomies named her "Georgetta."

The heavy-footed spirit who never showed his face was known as "George." They came to associate his noisy walk with the smell of incense. There was also a hint that George may not have been an animal-lover. The women had a pet cat who loved to roam across the kitchen counter, looking for scraps of food. On several occasions, when the cat attempted to jump to the counter top, it was batted away, as if by an invisible hand. Once, when the unsuspecting feline hopped into a chair, it appeared to hover approximately six inches above the seat for several seconds. Then, it was rudely ejected to the floor. It was as if it had landed on a most unwelcoming lap.

The four women were never frightened away by the specters but, eventually, their lives took them in different directions. Two left to marry, one went off to graduate school, and the fourth moved into a friend's Dallas apartment. That's when things got strange, even by ghost-story standards—because at least one of the spirits moved with her.

The first night the woman stayed in the apartment, her new roommate was kept awake by the strong smell of vanilla. Every time she closed her eyes, the scent wafted across her face. When she opened her eyes, it would vanish. This person had heard all of her friends' tales about their haunted house and had scoffed at every one of them. But, suddenly, she was not so sure.

The floor began to creak and groan where it never did before. There were numerous other strange noises, and unexplainable events occurred on a daily basis. Life in the apartment had always been quiet before, so the new roomies theorized that a ghost, or ghosts, had followed the one young woman from the other haunted house.

Why the spirits chose her over the other three room-mates is impossible to know. Perhaps she was the only one who stayed in Dallas. Perhaps she was the most sensitive to the paranormal. Or perhaps they simply liked her the best. After all, ghosts must surely have preferences, too.

The Humming Ghost

The Mistletoe Heights neighborhood in Fort Worth is rich in ambiance. The streets are wide and lined with trees. The sidewalks are illuminated with ornamental lights. The dwellings range from cottages to mansions, but all share the distinction of being part of a historically significant area. And what historically significant area worth its salt doesn't have a famous ghost?

This one is popularly known as "The Humming Ghost of Mistletoe Heights." She wanders through the halls and stairwells of one home in this neighborhood, crooning softly to herself. She has been seen by several people, including three former residents of the home, who independently produced matching descriptions of the phantom.

In the late 1980s, two local ghost hunters found the story so intriguing that they convinced the owner of the home to allow them to spend several nights there. They came armed with cameras and tape recorders and, on two occasions, a female psychic. During one séance the woman conducted, the ghost hunters claim to have encountered the spirit. They shared their notes with a reporter from the *Fort Worth Star-Telegram*.

"On the night of July 11, 1987 ... a woman's voice was heard by all three participants. Though we could not locate the voice, the three of us heard it coming from three different directions .... Our video and audio recorders did not pick up the voice."

It seemed that the trio had heard the famous phantom but did not see it. They had interviewed a former resident who had seen the apparition, however, and shared her strange story.

The woman said that the humming ghost like to spend time in "the pantry, the basement, and the stairwell coming up to the pantry from the basement." The spirit obviously felt strongly that these areas belonged to her. The lady of the house realized this when she awoke one night to find the apparition hovering beside her bed. The ghost was upset about some particular items of food that had been taken from the pantry. The woman replaced the groceries, and the ghost never appeared to her again.

She may have continued to hum for her, though—that haunting, unrecognizable tune that is this particular spirit's spectral trademark.

Miss Bettie Brown

There is a beautiful, historical mansion in Galveston that is called "Ashton Villa." It was built in 1859 by a wealthy businessman, James Moreau Brown, and was used to host many spectacular social events. Presiding over these parties was the master of the house and his colorful, gregarious daughter, Rebecca. The popular young woman was never called Rebecca, though. To one and all, she was known as "Miss Bettie."

To say that Miss Bettie was ahead of her time would be an understatement. While her Victorian counterparts were concentrating on propriety, Miss Bettie smoked in public, traveled unescorted and entertained a series of suitors. Other girls of the day practiced being demure, but Bettie Brown loved to be the center of attention—and often was, as she was an accomplished pianist and artist. Rumor has it that her outrageous behavior eventually caused a rift between the independent young woman and her father. The two never reunited, and when Miss Bettie eventually passed away, she was living alone in Europe, having been estranged from her family for several years. Today, however, there are many who believe that after her death, Miss Bettie's flamboyant spirit was drawn home to Galveston and her beloved Ashton Villa.

The three-story Italianate brick mansion was eventually restored to its original lavish state and turned into a museum. Caretakers were on hand to keep an eye on the expensive property at night. One caretaker, who lived in the Villa's carriage house, had an interesting encounter with Miss Bettie's spirit.

Miss Bettie Brown was unwilling to abandon the gaiety of her lovely home for the cold and quiet of a cemetery.

In an article written in 1978, the man explained that he had been awakened in the wee hours one morning by the tinkling sound of a piano. He threw on some clothes and went immediately to check the Villa. Once inside, he was certain that someone had broken in, for the music was louder and definitely coming from the antique piano in the main parlor known as the "Gold Room." The caretaker crept quietly along the corridor and silently unlatched the door, hoping to surprise the trespasser. Instead, as he stepped into the room, it was he who gasped in shock. Seated at the piano was the shimmering, semi-transparent figure of a woman dressed in Victorian fashion. It took only a moment for both the woman and the music to dissipate, but the impact of the experience stayed with the caretaker longer. He admitted that he did not sleep for the remainder of the night and turned on every single light to calm his nerves.

Was the spectral figure at the piano Miss Bettie? It seems to make sense. The Gold Room is splendidly appointed with many of her most cherished possessions, and music was one of her favorite pastimes. Other stories about this gentle spirit, though, indicate that she does not limit her haunting activities to this one room.

In the October 29, 1993, edition of the *Houston Chronicle*, Lucie Testa, a weekend manager of Ashton Villa, spoke of a number of ghostly happenings to which she had been privy. In one case, a volunteer reported seeing a woman in a dazzling turquoise dress, posing at the top of the grand staircase. Testa did not know of anyone whose costume matched the description. She did, however, know that turquoise had been Miss Bettie's favorite color.

Testa herself had experienced some unusual things in her opulent workplace. She noted that an extravagantly decorated chest that Miss Bettie had purchased while on one of her many travels tended to lock and unlock on its own. This was particularly mysterious because the key had been lost for years. There were stories of unexplainably rumpled bedcovers in Miss Bettie's bedroom and rumors of visitors to the house sensing that they were being closely followed by a "presence." And then there were the strange events of February 18, 1991.

Lucie Testa was becoming frustrated that day, as the Villa's alarm system had been triggered three times with no apparent cause. Then, just as she was leaving for the day, the ceiling fan at the top of the staircase began to make lazy circles in the air. Testa went upstairs to turn it off and then locked up for the night. The next morning, the fan was spinning once more. It was then that Testa realized the significance of the previous day's date. It was the 136th anniversary of Miss Bettie's birth. And, surely, anyone who loved a party as much as Miss Bettie Brown would not let her own birthday pass unnoticed.

The Old Castle

An interesting ghost story took place in the late 1960s in an Austin home sometimes referred to as "The Old Castle." Although many people seemed to know about the phantom even earlier than that, it was the experiences of Mr. and Mrs. Roy Winters that became most well known.

When the Winters were moving into the old, fortress-like home, some of their new neighbors came forward to warn them about the haunting. Mrs. Winters's positive response was likely not what they expected. "I was delighted," she told a writer for the *Austin American-Statesman*. "Now I had a 'castle' and a ghost to go with it."

It wasn't just any old ghost, either—this one came complete with a grisly legend. The story went that in the 1920s, when the house was vacant and undergoing some construction, a man murdered his young wife there. He then disposed of her lifeless body in the water tower, the oldest part of the building. Ever since, her lonely spirit had roamed through the rooms, seeking peace.

Mrs. Winters was eager to meet her resident specter, but for the first few months that she and her husband lived in the home, all was relatively calm. Her normally passive border collie acquired a strange habit of barking and growling at 2 AM, but nothing else was amiss. It wasn't until Mrs. Winters was alone in the house for the very first time that she experienced what she described as a "vision."

"It could have been a dream," she admitted in the Halloween, 1977, edition of the *Austin American-Statesman*, "but I don't think so. It was very lifelike." The newspaper story quoted Mrs. Winters's description of the events:

> she awoke at 2 AM to find she had a clear view of the stairway leading to the top of the old water tower. A wall, built since the 1920s, had mysteriously vanished. The room was suffused with a rosy light, apparently issuing from a window, and in the midst of a nebulous mass floated the face of a woman.

The apparition quietly approached Mrs. Winters and spoke a single sentence: "I am leaving you." It was the last thing that Mrs. Winters remembered before darkness overcame her. She later assumed that she had simply gone back to sleep.

The next morning, Mrs. Winters pulled out some canvas and brushes and, from memory, began to paint a portrait of the woman. It took several days to create the likeness. When it was done, Mrs. Winters had the painting hung in her living room.

For quite some time, the portrait was the only reminder that the Winters had of their ghost. Then, eventually, the spirit did make herself known again, though only on an annual basis. From that point forward, the paranormal activity tended to be less dramatic.

Mrs. Winters blamed the mysterious ringing of her door bell and unexplained opening and closing of her garage door on the spectral woman. Her husband blamed both on mechanical malfunctions. Mr. Winter did admit to having witnessed some puzzling events, however—such as the windless morning when he watched the patio swing moving back and forth, quite deliberately. And then there was the inexplicable event that took place during a party that the Winters hosted in early 1977.

A number of guests had asked Mrs. Winters to tell them her ghost story, and she was obliging. "I was halfway through the story," she said, "when one of the candles in the candelabra popped out of its holder and fell. When the florist we had rented it from came to pick it up, he was astounded. He said that never happens."

Chances are, nothing like that ever happened again in the home. The Winters eventually sold their haunted castle, and some years later, writer Rich Tharp interviewed the current residents. "We have not experienced anything that I would say borders on the supernatural," said the man. "We've got a 140-pound Newfoundland dog who is afraid of thunder, lightning and loud noises, and she's never given any indication that there's any fallen spirit here."

Perhaps, then, this is one famous ghost who is now at rest.

The Fabulous Ms. De Winter

In an era when being chic and entertaining lavishly were the highest aspirations of many women, Ms. Bert De Winter was envied and admired by all of Dallas society. The director of Neiman-Marcus's millinery boutique was famous for her fashion sense and her luxurious lifestyle.

"She lived very extravagantly, like a princess," one woman was quoted as saying in the October 31, 1982, *Dallas Morning News*. "Ms. De Winter had the finest of everything and did it all with the utmost taste."

One way Bert De Winter displayed her taste and wealth was by throwing the most magnificent parties of the day. She was known to be a fabulous hostess who routinely entertained the rich, famous and even royal visitors to the city. Guests knew that they would be treated to the very best of everything when they received an invitation to De Winter's splendid 14-room University Park home.

Bert De Winter took enormous pride in that home, decorating it throughout with expensive French antiques and carefully chosen accoutrements. The marble mantlepiece was purchased in Italy, the walls were covered in pink silk, and one room—with its black slate floor and red-and-white-striped chintz walls—was decorated to resemble New York's famous Peppermint Twist Lounge. Every decorative flourish in the mansion attested to the eminent fashion doyenne's personal sense of savoir-faire and style. Bert De Winter considered her home to be her ultimate accessory. It was hardly surprising to find that she may not have wanted to leave it.

Bert De Winter died in 1972, and her home sat vacant for a year. When Don and DiAnne Malouf viewed the house, with its handsome brick exterior and large flower gardens, they thought it had "immense personal charm." According to the *Dallas Morning News*, they were soon to find out "how personal the charm would be." They purchased the property and moved in in the autumn of 1974. Within days, the couple and their four children realized that they were not alone. In the *News* story, DiAnne Malouf described those first frightening experiences:

> The fourth or fifth night after we'd moved in, the whole house started creaking really loudly. At first we thought it was just the house settling.

> In the middle of the night, we heard someone walking through the dining room. It sounded like a slipper hitting the back of a foot against the wooden floor. All at once, the curtains in our bedroom stood straight out, and we could hear the children screaming and crying from their rooms.

> Don and I just clung to each other, frightened to death. We were too terrified to get out of bed and calm the children.

> We knew right away that it was her ghost. Something just told us that.

Bert De Winter had announced her continued presence in the house. In the days and weeks that followed, she demonstrated further that she was not prepared to leave. The distinctive footsteps and flying curtains occurred nearly every night, and the Maloufs began to sense the ghost's presence in every room of the house. Maybe she was objecting to the drastic changes that were being made to her home as the Maloufs undertook extreme renovations.

"I remembered that I had used a pick axe to dig up the black slate floor," DiAnne Malouf said. Seeing her adored Peppermint Twist Lounge treated in such a way must have enraged Bert De Winter. If she was angry, though, she sometimes had an odd way of showing it—for one of the ghost's habits was to leave pieces of her jewelry in various places around the house. It was never said whether or not the pieces were valuable, but, given Ms. De Winter's taste and wealth, they were unlikely to be faux.

The Maloufs often felt Bert De Winter's presence most strongly when they were planning to entertain. "She was always there when I was arranging a dinner party," said DiAnne Malouf. "It was as if she were saying, 'Let's see how you're doing today, DiAnne.' I never felt hostility from her, but she made it known to us that we could never compete with her extraordinary taste in decorating and entertaining."

There was only one occasion on which Bert De Winter's ghost showed itself to DiAnne Malouf. Not surprisingly, it was as DiAnne was formally setting the dining room table for guests. She told the *News* that she first felt the spirit near her, then turned and actually saw her. She noted with interest that the woman who had been so well known for her exquisite fashion sense appeared to be simply draped in a sheet, although it was "a French Porthault sheet—the most expensive kind."

The Malouf family was never able to become accustomed to the haunting. "We'd never stopped being frightened by it, but we would say to ourselves, 'What are we going to do?' We couldn't tell our friends or the police. They would have thought we were crazy."

The Maloufs didn't want to perform an exorcism; they were afraid of harming Bert De Winter's spirit. A cleansing ritual—an old folk remedy suggested by a friend—seemed to be a less violent solution to their paranormal problem. One night, during a dramatic thunderstorm, the Maloufs lit a dozen candles and sprinkled salt in the corners of each room. After the ritual, the ghostly activities seemed to subside, although the family could still sense that Bert De Winter was with them.

After four years, Don and DiAnne Malouf decided to sell their beautiful home. "The house was wonderful," said DiAnne, "but her presence was everywhere."

Their oldest child, Blake, agreed, saying, "I hated the house from the day we moved in, because it was always her house, not ours."

The Maloufs sold the house in 1978 to people who later reported that they did not once experience Bert De Winter's ghost.

It's a good thing. When you pay a half-million dollars for a house, you don't want it to come with a roommate—no matter how cultured she may be.

Chapter 7

A Strange
Assortment

Ghosts can be unpredictable, so there are many stories that refuse to fit into tidy categories. Equally frustrating is that any search for tales about spirits inevitably leads to a few strange-but-true accounts of other paranormal phenomena, which, while not exactly ghostly, are too good to leave out.

These are the eerie extras that have been woven into Texas's rich tapestry of supernatural legends.

Haunted by Himself

In May 1974, *FATE* magazine published a letter from a woman who lived in the small community of Bear Creek, near Cleveland, Texas. She described an event that qualifies as strange, even by ghost story standards.

According to the letter, many residents of one neighborhood in Bear Creek spent most of 1963 being "terrorized" by a stranger in a white shirt. The man harmed no one physically but would frighten people by appearing suddenly out of nowhere. No one recognized him, and no one knew what the trespasser wanted. The mere idea that an outsider was lurking around their homes and yards was disturbing, however.

When people began talking to one another, they discovered that there had been numerous sightings. One woman was on her way home from visiting a neighbor when she spotted the man standing in her yard. By the time her vehicle pulled up to the house, he had vanished. Two other residents reported having shot at the stranger. Obviously, though, they had missed. "Everyone had seen him at one time or another," wrote the woman, "but no one had gotten a look at his face."

One fellow who claimed to have twice seen the man in his own yard seemed particularly disturbed by the situation. He had become nervous, easily shaken and eventually was afraid to leave the house on his own. His family was concerned that he might be having a nervous breakdown, and their fears seemed to be confirmed by a strange confession he one day made to his wife.

The distraught man very suddenly announced that the

mysterious man in the white shirt was his own ghost.

"You can't be serious," said his wife.

"Just wait," he said. "Wait until the next time that fellow shows up in our yard, and I'll prove it to you."

A few weeks later, the wife saw the figure standing in the far corner of their large back yard. She told her husband, who, despite his debilitating agoraphobia, strode boldly out to meet the stranger. The anxious woman watched as her husband made a short speech and then turned confidently and marched back into the house. When she saw the pleased look on his face, she asked him what he had said.

"I told him, 'I know who you are,'" the husband said. "I said, 'You are my ghost. I'm tired of your terrorizing my neighbors, so go away and let them alone.'"

It seemed unbelievable, and the woman was likely sure that her husband had finally had the nervous breakdown that the family had been fearing. However, the fellow's mental state improved dramatically after that day, and no one in Bear Creek ever saw the stranger in white again.

Saved by Something

In December 1967, two sisters took their children Christmas shopping in Colorado City. On the way home, all was quiet in the car, as the youngsters slept in the back seat and the women happily reflected upon the purchases they had made. The group had been traveling in companionable silence for several minutes when the woman who was driving felt her sister tap her on the shoulder. "Pull over here, and stop immediately," she said.

The woman pulled the car over to the side of the road at the bottom of an extremely steep hill, then turned to ask her sister why she had wanted to stop. Before she could form the question, however, she saw that her sister was staring straight ahead, her face frozen in fear. The woman turned her attention back to the road and immediately saw the problem.

A huge truck-and-trailer unit had jack-knifed and was sliding sideways down the hill. The length of the truck covered both lanes of the highway, and it narrowly missed crushing the small car as it went skidding past. A short distance beyond, the massive vehicle veered off the road, hit an embankment and came to a sudden stop. The driver, unharmed, jumped out of the cab and ran over to check on the women. He was immensely relieved when he saw that their car had not been so much as scratched.

"Lucky you weren't coming up that hill!" he said. "The rig was out of control, right from the top."

It had been lucky, indeed. The two women sat quietly for a moment, gathering their wits. Finally, the driver said to her sister, "I don't know why you wanted to stop, but it sure saved our lives!"

The sister stared back in disbelief. "I didn't want to stop," she said. "I was about to ask you why you wanted to stop!"

"But you tapped me on the shoulder ... " The sister shook her head. The two stared at each other in wonder.

The woman later wrote, "It could not have been one of the children, for they slept through the whole terrifying experience. [But] whoever or whatever touched me that day saved our lives."

The Ghostly Rider

It was 1935, and the West Texas town of Wink was enjoying the earliest days of its oil boom. In the midst of the Depression, men were happy to have the jobs that the rigs provided, no matter how hard they were expected to work. On one particular job site, north of town, the roughnecks had to deal with something more than heavy labor, however. They had to cope with a ghost.

The specter would always appear in the cold, early mornings, just as the night shift handed things over to the daytime workers. The scene was described by Leon Thompson, in the Holidays 1996 issue of *Past Present Future.*

A strange Indian boy on a horse came riding through camp as fast as he could go. He looked straight ahead, but hoof beats and the boy's voice urging his charger to go faster could be heard. In seconds, both rider and horse had vanished into the mist around the camp, leaving an eerie silence.

During the latter part of the Depression, oil field workers near Wink were frequently spooked by the eerie specter of a horse and rider.

The oil field workers were intensely curious about the young phantom. They wanted to know who he was and where he was going. Eventually, they decided that they would try to stop him on his daily pass through the site.

They formed a plan, but it wasn't effective. The workers simply stood together in a line, forming a human barrier across the path that the rider usually took. The blockade didn't succeed in even making the boy pause—he simply rode his horse straight through the men. The workers weren't trampled, but they felt a rush of freezing air sweep across them as he passed. A number of men became so spooked at that point that they quit the jobs for which they had been so desperate. The ghost rider was more dedicated to his duty. Nearly every morning he continued to appear, coaxing his steed into a mad race across the oil field.

The boy was a supernatural fixture of the work site for four more years. In 1939, he made his last recorded appearance in the camp. He might have been forgotten if not for a gruesome discovery some 23 years later.

In 1962, pipeline workers near the original site of the rider unearthed a skeleton that had been buried in a seated position. They carefully exhumed the bones and then sent them for scientific testing. The results showed that the remains had been those of a Native American Indian male, approximately 16 years old. Everyone felt certain that he must have been the mysterious ghostly rider. After years of charging across the West Texas oil fields, the boy's existence had finally been confirmed.

X-ray Eyes

In the year 1900, Guy Finlay was a fourth-grader in Zavala County. Not an average fourth-grader, though, for Guy had discovered that he had a unique psychic ability: he was able to locate underground sources of water. In that dry ranch country, where new water wells were always needed to sustain life, this was a valuable skill indeed.

Guy first mentioned the strange gift to his father, Joel Finlay. "I can always use a new well," was the man's smiling response. When Guy told him that he had already marked the location for an excellent one on their property, Joel decided to take a chance. He paid some well drillers to bore a hole into the ground that Guy had marked. He even told the men that he had chosen the spot based upon nothing more than his son's "hunch." If the drillers had thought Joel Finlay was wasting his money, they didn't think that way for long. They had barely sunk into the ground when a cool stream of water came gushing forth. It was one of the best wells the drillers had ever brought in, and word of young Guy's find quickly got around.

Before long, Guy Finlay was known as "the boy with the x-ray vision." Ranchers came from far and wide to ask the psychic 10-year-old to find water on their properties. Guy was willing to do it, and his father was willing to let him do it—for a price. Before long, the cost of a well located by Guy's x-ray eyes was as high as $500. The Finlays probably thought that Guy was set to enjoy a lucrative, lifelong career as a seer. It didn't quite work out that way. Many decades later, an elderly Guy Finlay was quoted as saying, "The power lasted until my family started to commercialize on it. Then, it vanished."

One can suppose that the talent was like a well that simply dried up.

The First Wife

In these days of high divorce rates and blended families, there are numerous books, therapists and other resources available to help those who have trouble adjusting from one domestic situation to another. But what if you're having trouble with not an ex-spouse but a late spouse? It has been known to happen.

One Texas man suffered a great loss when his wife and baby daughter were killed in an accident. In time, however, he healed and began to see a few women socially. After all, he was a young man who hoped to rebuild his life. To him, that meant eventual remarriage, although his first wife had always expressed her disapproval of such a situation. "If I should die, promise me that you'll never remarry," she had pleaded with him. He never made such a promise, but the woman's wishes had been clear.

The day came that the man fell in love with a woman in her late twenties. They quickly became engaged and spent all of their time together, dividing it between his apartment and hers. Soon, they began to notice strange things happening in both homes.

There were strange noises: the sound of someone walking in the next room, the crash of heavy objects falling and mysterious knocking at the door. Every time the man or his fiancée would investigate, they found nothing. The window blinds began to snap open for no apparent reason. And books were often tampered with— a volume that was left closed would be flipped open to reveal certain passages when its reader returned. The couple had to admit that they were being followed by a ghost, and by the pages the spirit highlighted as clues, the man believed it to be his late wife.

The couple approached parapsychologist and author Hans Holzer for advice concerning their unique problem. He suggested that they should address the deceased woman and clearly explain the facts of "afterlife" to her. Whether that worked or not remains unknown. According to Holzer, the couple never contacted him again.

☠

Other widows and widowers have been fortunate in that their spectral spouses have been understanding, and even helpful, when the time came to move on. A fellow named Harold, a widower with five children, was blessed in that sense. He had been visited by his wife, Esther, several times following her death. When two years had passed, however, Esther appeared less frequently—and something amazing happened.

Harold was driving just outside of San Antonio when he stopped to help a woman repair a flat tire. They felt an immediate kinship and enjoyed a long, friendly conversation. Both were stunned when they discovered that they shared an important bond: the woman, Lydia, had been very close friends with Esther. Since the women had known each other through church activities, and Harold was not active in the church, Lydia had never met her dear friend's husband. As they sat by the highway, shaking their heads in amazement, Lydia and Harold realized that they had been "formally introduced" by Esther.

Not surprisingly, a romance blossomed, and the couple eventually married. The last time Harold saw Esther's ghost, he told her of his engagement to Lydia. The luminous apparition must have been satisfied, for she never appeared to her husband again.

The Accident That Didn't Happen

On October 5, 1969, Elston Brooks, an editor for the *Fort Worth Star-Telegram*, was driving his family to the State Fair in Dallas. At one point en route, Brooks checked his rearview mirror and saw a frightening sight: a white Chevrolet, traveling at highway speed, had suffered a tire blowout. The car had begun to fishtail wildly. Still hurtling along at more than 60 miles per hour, it careened back and forth across all three lanes of traffic. Other motorists had their eyes glued to the scene as they veered out of harm's way. There were at least five people, including Brooks, who watched in horror as the door of the Chevrolet flew open and the driver was thrown out on the pavement. The gruesome scene took one more turn for the worse, as the out-of-control car spun around and skidded over the body of its ejected driver.

"Don't look back!" Brooks instructed his family. He was sure that even he lacked the stomach necessary to survey the accident scene. Fortunately, he had spotted a police cruiser parked on the shoulder of the road ahead. Brooks pulled over and got out of his car.

"Is this about the accident?" the officer asked before Brooks had even had a chance to speak. He nodded. Apparently another driver had already flagged the police car down and reported the horrible crash. The officer jumped into his cruiser, set the siren wailing and roared back down the highway. The Brooks family carried on to spend their day at the fair, although not one of them was capable of enjoying it.

That evening, Elston Brooks found that he couldn't forget the incident, especially the mental image of the man being crushed by his car. He decided to get more information about it, so he called his office to see what details the *Star-Telegram* had been given. He was shocked to discover that they had no information about the accident whatsoever.

In the morning, when there was still no report at the newspaper office, Brooks called the police. What they told him was incredible: they had no accident recorded on file but did have statements from four other people who had seen the driver being thrown from his white Chevrolet. Brooks was confounded and asked to speak with the officer to whom he had reported the accident.

Patrolman David Fisher had been the cop at the scene. He had spoken to Brooks and one other motorist about the crash and had heard other reports of it come across his radio. When he had ventured back down the highway, however, Fisher found nothing out of the ordinary.

"There was a man and a white Chevrolet pulled over to the side of the road," he said. "The guy was fixing a flat." Aside from that, Patrolman Fisher had seen nothing to suggest that there had been an accident. He had turned around and headed back toward Dallas. As he retraced his route, he noticed that the car with the flat tire had gone on its way.

No one involved in the bizarre incident could offer an explanation, but Elston Brooks offered a vivid description. He called it "a horror story with a happy ending," and he couldn't have been more correct.

The Mysterious Marfa Lights

In 1883, 16-year-old Robert Ellison was working as a cowboy on a cattle drive way out in West Texas. The group had decided to camp overnight on the wide, flat terrain about a dozen miles east of the little community of Marfa. When night fell, Ellison had trouble sleeping, as he was concerned about the strange, flickering lights that he could see in the distance. When he pointed them out to others in his party, they shared his concern. "Those could be Apache fires in the mountains," someone said. But the next morning, a thorough search of the territory revealed no deserted camps. In fact, the group could find no explanation at all for the dancing points of illumination. It was a mystery and about to become a famous one. Today, Robert Ellison is considered to be the first white man to witness the Marfa Lights.

Marfa, Texas, is a community of some 3000 souls that sits about 100 miles northwest of Big Bend National Park. Its claims to fame are quirky and varied: Marfa was the filming location of the 1955 movie *Giant*, it boasts the golf course with the highest elevation in Texas (4688 feet) and it is home to the Marfa Lights.

Of those three attractions, the lights have proven to be the greatest tourism boon. Every year on Labor Day weekend, thousands of people flock to the area to take part in the "Marfa Lights Festival," an event complete with a parade, a rodeo, street dancing, food and plenty of discussion of the phenomenon being celebrated. Best of all for the town, the appeal of the lights is there the whole year long. The traffic has always been so steady, and local ranchers were becoming so frustrated by trespassers, that an official viewing area was built on Mitchell Flats, nine miles east of town on Highway 90. There, on any pleasant evening, dozens of curious people will gather to watch the supernatural show. Rarely are they disappointed.

There are cynics who like to say that the Marfa Lights are more about money than they are about mystery. Still, even those folks have to admit that the economic benefit would have vanished long ago if the paranormal phenomenon had not continued to intrigue. The lights are just too darned interesting and too hard to dismiss. They are dramatic, as well, rewarding those who visit the viewing area with a show that sometimes rivals a fireworks display.

The lights can appear as bright white or any number of vivid colors. People have seen brilliant green, yellow, red and orange globes floating and dancing in the night sky. Two separate points of light will sometimes merge together, or single lights will divide in two. They have been known to circle one another, move together in gracefully choreographed patterns, then shoot off in different directions. Sometimes a light will display a halo of coppery sparks or send off showers of blue and orange ones. The sightings are frequent, and they are never dull.

Today, most people watch the Marfa Lights from the designated roadside area, which looks out over an abandoned air base towards the distant Chinati Mountains. They have also been sighted from the air, however, by pilots who were confused by the strange "beacons." According to Michael Norman and Beth Scott in *Haunted America* (Tom Doherty Associates, 1994), the phenomenon was intensely investigated by both the air force and the army until the Pentagon issued a directive to "leave the lights alone."

No government order could ever keep people from speculating about the origin of this phantom fire, however. In the days long before Robert Ellison "discovered" the lights, Apache Indians believed the glowing orbs to be inhabitants of the spirit world. There were Natives and settlers alike who took the lights to be a sign that an executed Apache chief named Alsate was searching for his lost tribe. There is an enduring legend that explains the phenomenon as campfires from long ago, another that portrays the lights as witches or demons, and then there are the countless UFO theories. For every person who can put forth a supernatural theory, however, there are two who are eager to bring on the science.

The most common natural explanation for the Marfa Lights (and every similar phenomenon on record) is that they are simply the headlights of cars on a distant highway. Undoubtedly, this explanation accounts for some of the sightings, but not all. It could not explain the colored lights, the bouncing ones or those that were routinely seen before automobiles traveled the landscape.

One of the most interesting, and plausible, hypotheses is that the lights may be the result of the Novaya Zemlya effect, in which lights from distant sources have been refracted by the atmosphere and made to appear far from their sources. It is said that this effect could not be at work on overcast nights, however, and the Marfa Lights put on a fairly dependable show, come rain or (moon)shine.

Other suggestions have ranged from the mundane (ball lightning) to the ridiculous (jackrabbits that have been coated with phosphorous), with some reasonable-but-yet-to-be-proven theories falling in between. The truth is, in this case, the skeptics have had as little luck proving their hunches as have the believers in the paranormal. It was once said that finding the lights' origins was like trying to catch a rainbow. What causes the lights is a true mystery—and that's a large part of the appeal.

Richard A. Lovett wrote about the lights in the April 16, 1995, *Denver Post*. He said, "Whatever the explanation for the lights, the attempt to spot them brings one face to face with the realization that there are still many things that the modern world, for all its vaunted intellectual prowess, has yet to understand."

That, in a nutshell, may be why people love to go looking for the famous Marfa Lights.